# ROMANCE OPTIONS

First published in 2022 by
The Dedalus Press
13 Moyclare Road
Baldoyle
Dublin D13 K1C2
Ireland

www.dedaluspress.com



ISBN 978-1-915629-01-2 (paperback)
ISBN 978-1-915629-00-5 (hardback)



Dedalus Press titles are available in Ireland
from Argosy Books (www.argosybooks.ie) and in the UK
from Inpress Books (www.inpressbooks.co.uk)

Cover image: Olly Kava / Shutterstock

The Dedalus Press receives financial assistance from
The Arts Council / An Chomhairle Ealaíon.

# ROMANCE OPTIONS

*Edited by*

Leeanne Quinn and Joseph Woods

DEDALUS PRESS

# Contents

# INTRODUCTION

When we were invited by Dedalus Press last autumn to take on the task of editing an Ireland-based anthology of contemporary love poetry, there was a resounding 'Yes' from both of us. Frank Ormsby's *The Long Embrace: Twentieth Century Irish Love Poems* initially came to mind when first thinking about extant love poetry from Ireland. Published some thirty-five years ago it features an expansive selection of love poems ranging from Yeats to Ní Chuilleanáin. While still a fine selection, we wondered what had changed in the intervening years in terms of love and its expression in poetic form. We wondered also to what extent contemporary poets were still writing about love? In a time of social and political upheaval, and environmental crisis, was there still a space for romantic love in contemporary poetry? And, if so, what did this space look like? It was time to look at one of poetry's most established themes with fresh eyes, to see what 21st century poetry would make of love amidst the landmark changes that have taken place over the past few decades.

The most obvious change to Irish society in recent years has been the continued separation of church and state, the move to a society that no longer polices the romantic and intimate lives of its citizens. While Ireland is still recovering from the trauma of this policing, the changes we've seen in recent years, from the Marriage Equality referendum in 2015 to the successful repealing of the eight amendment in the referendum of 2018, confirm the extent to which our bodies and our intimate lives are becoming just that: our bodies, our intimate lives. Coinciding with these political changes are the enormous changes witnessed in terms of the prevalence of technology and social media in our daily lives. The ways in which we seek out love are intimately tied to the ways in which we now communicate socially.

This anthology was compiled via an open call that itself served two main purposes. We hoped that an open call would be precisely that – an attempt to democratise the often opaque and exclusionary world of poetry anthologies. The decision not to draw upon the extant love poetry of the Irish canon was thus a deliberate one: an open call of this kind appeals to the here and now, and creates a snapshot of the response of contemporary poets to one of the oldest themes. The considerable response to the call – from new, emerging, and established poets alike – suggests that any doubts about the validity of romantic love as an adequate and pressing subject for poetry today were unfounded. Poets are still writing about love. Lover and beloved still very much traverse the lines of the contemporary poem.

The poems in this anthology, in their diversity and range, show us what love in the 21st century is and can be about. The anthology's title was inspired by poems from two of our contributors, Eva Griffin and Mícheál McCann. Both poems are titled 'Romance Option' and carry dedications to the other's author. The poems take place in non-tangible landscapes, in virtual gaming environments where romance and intimacy still follow established real-world patterns of quest and pursuit. There's a vulnerability to the poems, as longing and desire persist in solitude, and the term 'Romance Option' comes to suggest something of the complex economics of love and intimate relationships in today's society. We loved the idea of two poets speaking to each other across the anthology. We pluralised the term not only to expand upon its original context, but to convey the multiplicity of experience reflected in these pages.

While we want the poems here to speak for themselves, taken together they present a cross-section of the core concerns of the 21st century love poem, with poems of desire, of the body, of compromise, of satisfaction, of dissatisfaction. The poems here speak of language, its adequacies and inadequacies as a medium for the expression of love. They speak of loss and gain, of joy, of celebration. They speak of community, of identity. They speak of the past, of the present, and of the future. In short, these poems speak of love, and, in these challenging times for so many, in defence of love.

*— LQ & JW*

## Tomorrow

I give you the light behind my eyes,
it was yours before I was ever born.
I would count the reasons that you own it,
but there are fewer stars in the desert sky.

The only gift I can give to you
are promises that can be broken by me.
The only gift you can give in return
is that song you sing about hope's resolve.

When you have grown beyond my understanding
and wandered away into vivid colours,
your memory is the thing I will rest upon,
as my days begin to dip behind the hills.

Even then I will keep our fragile covenant,
that sweet imperative and law of love,
my dreams sinking like rain into the sand,
you still up ahead waving me on.

JOSEPH ALLEN

## Dorothea

And that is where they found you,
in your beloved garden,
one cheek dusted with soil.

Long summer evenings
I'd sit, half reading a paper,
watching you tend your plants,
weeding flower beds, edging the lawn,
years of intimacy
making conversation unnecessary.

Returning after your burial
I walk through the silent rooms,
windows closed to the winter chill,
unable to explain
the smell of freshly cut flowers.

BEBE ASHLEY

## Sappho, who is doing you wrong?

Even in another time, someone somewhere
will remember us.

Even in another time, swift sparrows
stretch over salt sea to the loveliest stars.

Even in another time, the dawn light scatters
your laughter glittering on this coal-black earth.

Even in another time, my wild soul here
like a hyacinth in the mountains.

Even in another time, I want to say something
but shame sends me stuttering.

Even in another time, Sappho,
who is doing you wrong?

Even in another time, I am weary
of your words, and your soft, strange ways.

AMANDA BELL

## Valentine

> *'So short our lives, so hard the lessons, so difficult the tests, so sudden the final victory, so tenuous the hope of joy that so easily evaporates into fear – this is what I mean by Love.'*
> —*The Parliament of Fowles,* Geoffrey Chaucer

The feeders empty faster now. Sparrows and blue tits are constant presences. A robin waits beneath, avidly pecking the chipped nuts that spray down like dust from a carpenter's saw. Emerging bulbs vanish, plucked cleanly from the soil. Goldfinches congregate nervously in the apple boughs, make forays to the sunflower seeds near the back door. A pair of woodpigeons ambles along the garden path, grazing in the borders more purposefully than before. A female blackbird combs the patio, dipping into each crack and fissure for grubs. High in the plum tree two bullfinches gleam pink as they bob, feasting; I would like to think on insects, but I suspect on buds. Day and night a magpie couple noisily debate the renovation of their nest.

dinner for two –
raised out of his tank, the lobster
running, running

MAUREEN BOYLE

## Cydnus

Plutarch says that when Antony arrived
to feast with Cleopatra
he was dazzled by an array of lights
he'd never seen before
hung from the top of her house
in every colour and shape imaginable.
She had curated a set on which to shine,
where darkness was banished
and light was somehow got in every place,
devices so artificially set
that this seasoned soldier, who had eaten
berries from the winter trees
and supped the stagnant water of puddles,
was bewitched and speechless.
What was so different here
from the grand houses of Rome he was used to?
What tricks of mirrors and of floating wicks,
what burning alabaster
made a sanctuary of the place
and lit the ceiling like a littoral sky swept with stars?
He craned his neck to gaze upon it,
even as his feet sank
into the depths of Paestum roses,
and she performed her magic trick
of taking the orb of pearl from her ear,
a full moon held between her fingers,
and dropped into a goblet,
to announce an eclipse
and the coming of the dark.

NICK BOYLE

## Clementines

are the type of fruit to be lightly
thrown and caught at cloudless picnics.

None could be found
and it was no matter.

The weather looked more bread and soup.

On the road to St John's Point Lighthouse,
foam fleeced the sea,

waspish stripes rang against purple,
ragdoll gulls, a rain-cut beam.

Even for us, schooled in brisk summers,
make-the-best-of-it summers,
stiff northern summers,
it was a brave day for a drive.

We resignedly ate, dabbed
napkins and sat awhile,
your hand held upon my thigh
as it roared and wailed outside.

"Well, at least it isn't snowing."

It began to hail.

I catch your laughter as clearly
as I heard it, clear as the ticking
clock on the wall,

thrown so lightly,

sweet and clean as a clementine.

DYLAN BRENNAN

## Stoneflower

Away from the acid-mustard glow
of sulphur crystals, Yves Klein crumble
of azurite, translucent bars of gypsum,
fruit pastille glisten of quartz lumps,
nestled in a room of drab cabinet fossils
between animal-pebbles from Iowa
and Devon, one I can never give to you.
300 million years ago slowly trapped,
mid-Carboniferous drop in sea level
dug up in what is now still Ireland –
*actinocrinus stellaris*. Strange to say
in encyclopaedias and online archives
I can find next to nothing other than
this: extinct genus of the crinoid,
from the Greek: *krinon-eidos* – form of a lily.

ELLEN BRICKLEY

## Midweek

I want to tell you a story.

It is Tuesday – except
it isn't really Tuesday,
I'm just telling you it's Tuesday so you won't imagine
Mondayish vigour, Fridayish hope;
instead you'll understand the middleness of Tuesday,
of life, when nothing happens –
and I say my goodbyes to carpet tiles, to
to the space between my feet.

"I miss you. I'm sorry.
Would you like a cup of coffee?
What can I bring you?
Is it too late?"

I don't really mean a cup of coffee –
I don't care for coffee, or about it –
but I want something hot and wakeful between us,
a morning ritual, a hard beating heart,
that can pass between your hand and mine,
that a flowering of early tweets
can call vital.

Sometimes you can't tell
by the shadow of a potion
passed between hands
that love went with it.
Some things are too strong for coffee.
They need to brush your fingers,
cannot penetrate an insulating sleeve.

You should learn, if you can, to recognise those things,
so you don't have to beg forgiveness
on a fake Tuesday
of your indifferent shoes.

CHARLOTTE BUCKLEY

## Louisburgh

All week the gorse bushes have been on the turn
and I have been at the sea house without you.
Though it is too early in the season for flowers,
I pass hours among the hedgerows waiting
for the first yellowing, days along the beach
collecting cowrie shells that I might divine what will happen
on my return. I listen to the songs of oystercatchers
which can be heard from here to Silver Strand,
wanting, of all things, for you to hear them too.

There are still days between us, still hours to be spent
beach picking and watching for yellow. I will write down
the songs, so I may sing them again when we are together,
as you stand on the roadside, or the pavement's grey,
and hear the birds coming in off the Atlantic,
see the gorse bush flowering at last.

## Cómóradh Pósta

*Ó tá sé ráite, adúradar,*
*Go ngiorraíonn beirt bóthar,*
*Téanam scathaimhín*
*Ag válcaeireacht lena chéile.*

Rianaíodar cosán, idir réidh
Agus rite, garbh agus mín,
Thar ardán, thar bhogach, go dtí –
Tar éis caoga bliain – gur lúb sé

Aniar aduaidh orthu
Go bhfuil an cosán sin i gcónaí
Chomh fada, chomh gearr
Le coiscéim isteach sa tsíoraíocht.

PADDY BUSHE

## Wedding Anniversary

*Since the wise ones hold,* they mused,
    *That company shortens the road,*
*Let us two, for a while,*
    *Go rambling together.*

They traced a path, between gentle
    And steep, rugged and easy,
Over high ground, across slough, until –
    After fifty years – at a bend that swung

Suddenly back on itself, it struck them
    That their path always has been
Just as brief, just as longlasting
    As a step into the eternal.

DAVID BUTLER

## Imbolc

Sick to death of the self
trapped
in breath-damp fabric,

the hour is at last
            propitious
to emerge the calyx;

                    to love,
take joy where one can
            randomly,

as a breeze teases
white-tops
from a puckering lake;

                    as a bee
stumbles across the face
of a dandelion.

DARAGH BYRNE

## And What of Love?

And what of love, that vast and splendid thing
That eats her young, while teaching them to sing?

ALICIA BYRNE KEANE

## Tapestry

*after Stardew Valley*

I will find you when the landscape glows teal at dusk.
A road unfurls to the village, one straight line.
I will have spent so long clearing a path to the orchard,
raising wholeness from the ground.
The days pass in minutes, downpour beautiful on a roof.
The scene blinks itself shut when I take new paths.
I am no stranger to reorientation:
in the bigger world,
it is only two days since I left your house.
Already, there has been so much news.
There is whale-song here only when it rains.
I wish we could send each other small channels of light
as we resist our respective fatigues;
I wish I was clear on the current quest.
Maybe there will be an axe slick in the grass,
something to make me stumble:
footsteps echo on the bridges
as I am carried from one gentleness of sand to another.
Slog slow as the light fades; ground narrowing by the pond.
Now I am not far from home. I miss you already,
located as you are offscreen.
You would almost forget how the scenes connect.

LORRAINE CAREY

## Palomino

I would have bought you a Palomino
fourteen hands tall,
had I the wherewithal to pay,
but ultimately love was not enough.
We'd have found a meadow together
or rented a farmer's field, heady
with just threshed hay, anything
to keep you here, a reason for you to stay.

Only horses with dark skin wear white coats
in winter. With her blessing I took
from your grave, the Palomino you made
at pottery class. *It's cracked in half from frost*
*but there's always glue,* she said
and slowly walked away, smaller than before.
The butterscotch glaze and creamy mane
still kiln shiny from years ago,

despite hoar frost and cemetery snow;
how you hated being cold.
The horse's head now on my wall,
its hairline crack, a wispy thread,
the subtlest of reminders that we can
never really know a person at all.

Your stables and Palominos lost
to a toy heaven in an alternative sky
with my Sindy doll amputees
and your Tiny Tears with dimpled knees,
where vapour trails spear cirrus wisps
fading like the ghostly swish of a horse's tail.

ANGELA T. CARR

## Quadratic Love Song

So many things will sit inside a square –
a book, a bell, a tooth, a cup, a bone –
but who would look and think to find them there?
Who'd ink their shape in light when there was none?
I think about the square that is a house,
a room, where footsteps creak the wooden boards –
the one that's empty of the two of us –
I'd name the sound if I could find a word.
Though you were never one to fit a tongue
or root equations as are graphed by hand –
you'd lay your shadow as your sun demands
and slip through pauses tighter than a drum.
My arms have learned to love the weight of air,
to circle what can't linger in a square.

ANNE CASEY

## Love in a time of chaos, a cento

*after James Joyce*

I hear an army charging upon the land,
thunder of horses plunging, foam about their knees:
arrogant, in black armour, the charioteers come out of the sea,
run shouting by the shore their battle-name: clanging, clanging
upon the heart as upon an anvil.

Earth and heaven tremble, vast wings above the lambent waters brood –
a waste of water sways, uplifts its weedy mane, and the dark rain falling,
wind whines and whines the shingle, each single slimesilvered stone.
As the twilight turns, the lamp fills with a pale green glow:
a birdless heaven, seadusk, one lone star piercing the west,
paler than time's wan wave – the voice of winter at the door.
Sing about the long deep sleep, leave dreams to the dreamers:
the time of dreaming, dreams is over.

Desolate winds assail with cries the shadowy garden where love is,
the moon a web of silence in this witchery. Sad as the sea-bird
going forth alone, the winds cry to the water's monotone,
the grey winds are blowing where I go.

When over us the wild winds blow, lightly come or lightly go
at the hour of evenstar as ghostfires from heaven's far
arch on night's sindark nave, the trysting and the twining star –
all night a veil, for love at first is all afraid.
Hurry over the dark lands and run upon the sea
for seas and lands shall not divide us –
you, my love and me.

Come, blind me with your kiss, bend deeper on me,
take me, save me at that hour when all things have repose.
Eastward the gradual dawn prevails – tremble all those veils:
do you hear the night wind sigh at that hour
when soft lights come and go
in the air above and in the earth below.

*This poem is constructed entirely of line fragments from poems by James Joyce.*

EILEEN CASEY

## Love in the time of Abba

*for John*

You admired my yellow cardigan.
Said it reminded you of a canary in dimly-lit
pubs and snooker halls around Rathmines,
sound-tracked by *Fernando* or *Dancing Queen*.
Late night suppers in The Gigs Place; greasy fries
followed by hung-over Sundays, sleeping 'till noon.

I adored your dark hair. Shades of a raven's
blue-black wings. Traces still shadow the grey.
The way you held your cue, squint-eyed, hip-
swivelled. The soft kiss of the snooker ball
before powering into the pocket.
You smoked cigarettes down to the tip. How
you lived life, nothing wasted. All that zest
transferred to fatherhood. *Chiquitita,*
*I have a Dream*; muted beneath crying babies.
Mostly, it was *you* rose in the early hours.
Changing nappies. Comforting toddlers.
New Age Man. Before that term was invented.

Love is different now. We rise early on Sundays,
vegetables and roast prepared the night before.
Pinned to the fridge, emergency phone numbers,
grand-children's rosy drawings. Framed
under glass, glory days of youth brighten
our twilight years. We still listen to Abba.
*I do, I do, I do, I do, I do.*

LOUISE G. COLE

## Seeing as I am Blinded by the Truth

I choose the long drive home, past
the lies of roadside rags I make out as
a traffic-butchered badger, close to
black flapping bale-wrap, grass-verged,
a car-crashed crow, still twitching. Or not.
And that dirty white Gull, broken-winged,
fluttering against barbed wire, in reality
a sodden square of old newsprint.

Flighty brown leaves scatter across
my path as mice and rats. They run
to the gatepost outline of an evil
monster, which could be you, though
it is hard to see, salt water blurring
my vision before I get as far as
the damaged dog in the gutter – a knot
of takeout wrappers, their whimpers
riding the winds of your rejection.

When I stop again, it is for the plastic tote
of river-banked kittens, drown-ready,
which I reveal as a litter-lout's leavings,
a bag of kitchen waste: tabby grey potato
peelings, ginger Tom scraps of carrot,
black cat turnip tops, rotting, the smell
unexpected, as if of you. But the sound,
the sound is that of a pathetic mewling,
which I recognise, and I am not mistaken.

SHIA CONLON

## Frank

it could be funny
how much we survived,
apart
it could be funny
how much we endured,
elsewhere
but
thinking of you
as a small child
alien,
cowboy,
not of earth
it feels serious
that of all the places
your body
could have roamed
you ended
up
here,
near me
and we share;

rooms
headquarters
dreams
a mission

the forest of your childhood
looks the same
as the one of mine
when you moved a branch to let in light
i saw the same sun

STEPHANIE CONN

## Making Beef Stew from Scratch

The days grow short.
You peel and chop potatoes,
prepare the stock. Beside you
I cut carrot and onion, drop
them into the pot. When you add
the bay leaves I ask if you know
the story of Daphne and Apollo?

You smile your crooked smile,
set the stew to simmer, lead me
out into the garden. The trees
are Birch and Ash and Oak. We
take cover from the drizzle. You
pull me into your arms under
the largest oak, kiss me against
bark, promise me the arrow
that pierced your heart was gold,

and while you would follow me
as far as Crete, or further still,
a single word from my lips
will halt any ill-fated pursuit:
the choice to stay or go will
always be my own. I quiver
in the bow of your embrace.

EMILY COOPER

## It has become one of those days

*Paris, August 2020*

when you speak more to the wasps than to me –
swear at them as they clamber inside your can of coke.
We are resting together on the bench –
weary but not quite done yet.

You swat at them anxiously, trying not to aggravate.
Your body in the heat is large and your muscles warmed
from all the walking. I lay my head on your shoulder,
your chin comes down gently to pause for a moment
before you're off again kicking out aggrieved and so content.

POLINA COSGRAVE

## A Test to Love the World

I wake up where my face meets the broken light.
I wake up and think of you. Then everything makes sense.

If the world contains such a living breathing miracle, perhaps it
can be loved.
If my head contains this line, it must be tested.

Everyday is a test to love the world.
Everyday I fail the test.

When I fail the test, I lie to the light.
When I lie to the light, it breaks.

If I break all the light in the world, you will make some more.
That's what living breathing miracles do.
If the world can be loved, the light can be fixed.

I wake up where your perfect light meets my broken face.
I try to fix it, so it reminds you of love.

I lie to the light that I live to make you smile.
The light remains whole.

DEREK COYLE

## Carlow Poem #81

When you cannot look away,
and you are wearing the sun
like a new shirt. It's springtime
and I want to take the sun
in hand, and open it up
like a new book. And I find you
in it. Surprisingly,
on the first page of the first chapter.
I can detect
your distinctive scent
mingled with that of the fresh paper,
the light cardboard of the cover.
You are the question mark
at the end of the first paragraph.
Set there by the printer,
with no knowledge of you.
It feels like the air was rationed all winter
and now it's arrived with the iced water
and the thinnest slice of lime.
I think of your hands,
how soft they are for a man. And, I appreciate
how often I've let go of you.
How, so like a man,
I don't think of you here,
in this world, in my life.
Until I saw you in the sun,
so unexpectedly, that it opened up,
to you, on a page in its book.

ENDA COYLE-GREENE

## Anniversary

13870 (quadrennial leaps left out)
ah – but who's counting?

BERNIE CRAWFORD

## I've Been Missing You

Our summer days always sparkled
with visits to your place
at Cor na Ron, the seal's beach.

My two girls found their seal skins with you,
straight into the curling waves they circled, you centred
selkies, mermaids, dolphins.

Later all snuggled in blankets and scarves,
we cooked mackerel over a smoky bonfire,
ate it falling between our fingers.

In lean times we made concoction soup.
Every withered vegetable in the basket
was scraped clean, chopped together
with out-of-date knobs of garlic.

We spread Nutella on cream crackers,
sprinkled desiccated coconut,
served it up with silver spoons, white linen napkins.
You always did it posh.

In recent years we had crab claws, scallops,
your famous date tart.
You blasted us with Edith Piaf
as we talked the kitchen into a spin,
danced saucepans off the stove.

Our laughter ricocheted off the large window
open to the sea where last winter
your daughter sprinkled your ashes.

I've been missing you
so the other morning when I went into the sitting-room
I wasn't at all surprised to find you there.

A slant of sunlight got caught in a piece of your stain glass
and threw a water colour on the opposite wall
of blue-green seas, rust-gold mountains.

PHILLIP CRYMBLE

## In Your Small Dream

It's warm. You ride the train to town together.
She's young. Her dress
is white and green. In life she works a day job

in Geneva. Ten years
ago you met again. As children once her family
came to visit. The others

teased her awkwardness. In the back seat
of the car you talked
for hours. She left. You think you loved her

then. The dream
unfolds like pretty paper flowers. The train back
home won't come.

You have to wait. The tracks are overgrown. The sun
seems tired. She takes
your hand. You know you're not awake. It feels

as if there's something
that needs saying. You stir. She sings to calm you.
You're afraid.

CATHERINE ANN CULLEN

## Subsidence

I did not know the weight of a heart
could sink a house. But where the front door
stood, only the lintel looms above ground now.

Today I squeezed onto the landing floor,
climbed down to where you slump in the cellar.

But we had no cellar. Here at the countertops
we drank the sun for years, with coloured straws
bent to savour the last drops.

Soon I'll take the children to the attic
to breathe some light. There the sun will set
in the window and the houses opposite
reflect the morning.
                                        When the rays get
to your heart, my love, they're bound to shift it.

I'd carry you up myself if I could lift it.

EMILY CULLEN

## Your Old Letters

Although we parted ways decades ago
I keep your letters bundled in a clutch
of envelopes tied in a satin bow
inside a box I don't return to much.

It doesn't matter that I don't reread
your phrases: some mundane, some fervid
they're still there and I must accede
I never struck a match, have not averted

from the fact you were my first true love.
All these years later, when we've both moved
on, with our spouses and children, you're still
in the gristle of my heart, the welter

of a cryptic chamber. And, it's odd to write
but true: no matter what, you'll remain there.

YVONNE CULLEN

## And the bird-shit ogham

And the bird-shit ogham
reflected in a flat roof's familiar puddle
told me how much I could love.
And every red brick in this view from a window.
Under the river of the afternoon, all
was perfect as a model. All my loves
were in that view:
nesting love: warm wood or wicker, lit behind windows,
and love for you:
shadow of an almost invisible bird,
beating, now like a heart, here, up a wall;
now: a girl swung in at an entryway
in yellow satin.

MARTINA DALTON

## Because Her Wedding Had to Be Postponed

What I think of now is how, on that morning
underneath the cherry blossom tree
you planted as a child,

a blackbird gathered bits of moss
her mate had plucked
and left to dry.

Confetti drops of petals
that were strewn,
she brought them to her nest.

And the photo that you posted online,
of the little branch, that he
had walked for miles to find.

How you'd placed it in the jug
you'd brought back from Japan.
And the simple cloth you lay it on.

Above the both of you, the firmament
without a single aeroplane
bringing newlyweds away, or coming in.

The blue and empty sky – unscarred.

MAUREEN DALY

## Swan

Grass in the park is a soft green
buds appearing on the skeletal trees.

I admire you
standing on the edge
of the pond
a lost partner,

your neck held high
above the ducks and gulls
frowning at their want for crumbs.

PHILIP DAVISON

## Bowl of Fruit

The suspended coal burst of a kiwi fruit.
I have never seen you eat a kiwi.

Where are you, my brother
in your coma?

I am not a ventriloquist
I will not tread softly to your bedside
I will organise no gathering.

Aren't you worried about me?
The birds are singing.
In all humanity
there is no mistake here.

This way, this way.
My daughter, not yet born,
will paint your nails.
I will peel an apple for you
from your lousy still life.

Listen to me.
The hearing, I know, is last to go.

STEPHEN DE BÚRCA

## Pomegranate Seeds

*What's the most important thing*
*you've done*
*with your hands?* you asked me
over mugs of lohikeitto.
Pomegranate seeds,
those little bulbs
of matter in the fish soup, were
your touch. Later, we took turns
rolling dice. I rolled
the nyyppä-yahtzee*
and you forced a smile
that ladled out the past
and future in equal parts
before we dozed
by the log-fire I set
that morning. The oak
was cut to size and
left to dry in the shed
the winter before we met –
those evenings called for
warmth in the absence
of spring light.

**Finnish: noob's yahtzee i.e. rolling five ones*

## Dráma Deireadh Caidrimh

Suíonn tú in aice leis san fhoscadán is breathnaíonn
ar an mbáisteach ag stealladh anuas, na tonnta á slogadh siar.
Ní labhraíonn ceachtar agaibh. Níl mórán le breathnú air
seachas an bháisteach is graifítí gnéasorgán
ar na ballaí, adharca ar na cinn fhireanna.

Cé a d'fhéadfadh a leithéid a tharraingt is cén fáth?
Ar theastaigh uathu preab a bhaint astu siúd, cosúil libh féin,
atá sáinnithe ag an mbáisteach, nó astu siúd
a théaltaíonn isteach faoi scáth na hoíche, seal suirí á lorg acu?
Suirí an rud deireanach atá ar d'intinn.

Tá ráite aige go bhfuil sé ag dul thar lear.
Go bhféadfaidh tú teacht in éindí leis
nó fanacht ina dhiaidh. Ní theastaíonn uait
an t-aon duine a bhfuil cion aige ort a chailliúint.
Ach má tá cion aige ort, tuige nach bhfanfaidh sé?

De réir mar a shlogann an fharraige an bháisteach, feiceann tú
eisean á shlogadh ag a bhfuil á mhealladh trasna na dtonnta.
I gceann de na longa úd a sheolann thar d'fhuinneog san oíche.
Í lasta suas. Long a mbíodh sé de rún agat taisteal inti.
Anois beidh an long sin ag breith do leannán léi.

A rogha déanta aige, tá sé ag fanacht go dtiochfaidh tú
ar chinneadh. Ní ghlacann sé rófhada ort é sin a dhéanamh.
Is ionann an rud atá á bhreith uait agus an rud
atá do do choinneáil anseo. É siúd ar mó é ná an grá
atá agaibh dá chéile – an gá bhur mbealach a dhéanamh sa saol.

CELIA DE FRÉINE

## Drama of a Break-up

You sit beside him in the shelter and watch
the rain pour down, the waves lap it up.
Neither of you speaks. There is little to look at
apart from the rain and graffiti of sex organs
on the walls. The males' in a state of arousal.

Who could have drawn such and why?
Did they hope to shock those, like you,
stranded by the rain, or those who creep in
under cover of dark for a spell of lovemaking?
Lovemaking is the last thing on your mind.

He has told you he is going across the sea.
That you can come with him
or stay behind. You don't want to lose
the only person who cares for you.
But if he cares for you, why not stay?

As the sea swallows the rain you see him swallowed
by what is bringing him across the waves. In one
of those ships that sail past your window at night.
All lit up. A ship you often dreamed of travelling on.
And now this very ship is taking your beloved away.

He has made his choice and is waiting for you to make yours.
It does not take long for you to decide. What is taking him
away is what is keeping you here. That which is bigger
than the love each of you have for the other – the need
to make your way in the world.

Agus na smaointe sin ag suaitheadh i do chloigeann,
coinníonn tú ort ag breathnú ar an mbáisteach.
An bheirt agaibh frámáilte i gceathrú balla an fhoscadáin,
a thugann cuireadh dóibh siúd ar muir breathnú ar stua
bhur gcruacháis, ach a ndíchreideamh a dhíbirt roimh ré.

As you turn these thoughts over, you keep
watching the rain. The two of you framed
by the fourth wall of the shelter that invites
those at sea to observe the arc of your dilemma.
Having first suspended their disbelief.

PATRICK DEELEY

## Paraphernalia

He carries a tray of tea and marmalade toast
shakily uphill, over shrubs
and bluebells, along the narrow pebbly path
and through gingery darkness
which the wedge-headed, red wooden box
that is my studio seems to exhale.
He's not the same man as stooped to pick me
a basket of wild strawberries
on a roaring hot day once upon a fairy-tale
in the Basque Country, nor even
the man from a few decades later, a mess
of honey from a hive in Italy
dripping off his hands – honey, I exclaimed,
about to tuck in; well, whatever
next – the prick of some poor, dying bee?
Not the man with black fingernails
and a farmer's wiriness, who turned a quarry
into a garden, wasps roused
from their disrupted nest weaving a corona
about his tattered sunhat
until, stung and stung again, he burst in here
to the catch of my arms. Not
any man but today's – wrinkles creaturing
his face, hair thinned, tea and toast
held before him as he comes
touching open the door into a cavern of colour,
of paraphernalia old as my wedding
to him: bric-à-brac, food mixers, hot pots
and stew pans, "magic" marmalade cutters
from a flipped kitchen dream – all
that's waited in the dark for just this fetch-back
by which I clear my way to art:
a cavort, a juggle, a canvas made to dance.

MAURICE DEVITT

## Unspoken

*for Teresa*

It must have been long before we met
that you learned the sorcery of silence –
how words only matter when they matter,
and how the breathless scram of conversation
sometimes does little but distract the senses.
I remember one time driving to Connemara,
you said nothing until just outside
Kinnegad – then merely to remind me
how the motorway spurs and not to miss
the turn. I had started the journey
with a skittish collage of jokes
and useless facts, intended to impress
my captive audience, but even these
quickly trailed off into quiescence –
the car a hide from which to stalk
the passing beauty, our breath measured
and perfectly in sync, eyes on fire
and your lips carved into a blissful smile.

PATRICK DILLON

## Madonna of the Pint Glass

So near me on the world that night
Your words increased me, one by one,
Carter, Hartnett, ruebob, arsehole,
They strum and thrum.
Extraordinary talker, plump swallower
Of daylight and plum curtains.
What am I to do with your legends
Now that all of you are gone?
The father. The mother. The broken bones.
The light bulb in the hallway and what
Happened in the hallway. The shards
Of laughter, the words pushing, turning
Till they were froth.

## $30^{th}$ Wedding Anniversary

In nature it is one
in every ten thousand;
tiny crystals, laid down
as swirled concentric layers
beneath shell and mantle
in soft, living tissue.

What were our chances?
Yet here we are. Inside
our marriage and around
the grit of day to day
we have grown – beautiful
and shining – this pearl.

DARREN DONOHUE

## Faraway fields are too green and there's a bull in one of them

The internet provider promises me more speed than ever before but I want to discuss Picasso. I want to talk about Picasso losing interest in his children because they grew up. The internet provider promises we can discuss all that and more after I sign the contract. But I tell him that Picasso once said he wanted to learn to draw like a child and everyone thought it was a lovely thing to say. He painted with his children, studying them. But the moment they realised their father was famous and studying them, he discarded them.

The internet provider nods but says nothing. Encouraged, I continue 'You see them in videos, Picasso and his children, on the beach in Nice. He's throwing them in the air, surrounded by sunlight. He's enthralled by them, mesmerized by them. And the children are pulling his ears or ignoring him, playing in the sand surrounded by sunlight. Picasso can't take his eyes off them. He's besotted. Bewitched.'

The internet provider scratches his ear and consults his clipboard. 'Imagine how his children must have felt,' I continue, 'one day being pushed away through no fault of their own. Imagine the intensity of Picasso's love and then imagine that love suddenly withdrawn. No, it wasn't love. How could it be love? Love persists. The love between a parent and child.'

'We're all children of the internet now,' sighs the internet provider, holding out his pen. I sign Picasso on the dotted line and we leave it at that.

KATHERINE DUFFY

## Choosing from the Archipelago

We relied on *The Rough Guide*,
wrestled ferry schedules.
Piraeus was a purgatory you had to pass
through. There were so many

dragons sleeping in a dark blue sway,
so many sunsets limning bays.
We were looking for *isychia**
which seemed to promise
something akin to *uaigneas.*

No rooms when we arrived;
we slept on the shore,
your skin warm through all the hours,
pebbles patterned my back.
I woke in fright at a long, eerie
hiss, reminder of a ship's passing.

We swore we'd take the next boat
but somehow held on, and on.
A slow-burn affair: the small
port in the lee of the mountain,
the high, enigmatic town,
built to bewilder pirates.

*ησυχια – *Greek for solitude, quiet, remoteness*

RORY DUFFY

## Half Life

In Miyagi prefecture, Mr. Takamatsu is slim
and weathered and moves towards the sea.
He has slipped into a new tight skin,
learned a new way to haul breath,
grown the steel of a tank on his ageing back.
Now his breath is bottled-up,
compressed, liquid and flat,
his face encased in a quick-silver bullet of light.
He slips his carapace into the radiant waters
to search the energised remnants of
tumbled rags and undone bodies.
He is un-coupled from the land
as he barbles through the gravel
of her gravity-thin world.
Above his head the atrium of cobalt water
swirls and circulates, beats and contracts,
the waves now un-monstered.
The sea is his chamber,
the weight of it a relief from the heavy water
that lies above his compressed thoughts.
He will swim and dive and probe,
he will creep and prod
and he will find Yuko.
One deep day his hand will touch hers,
he will exhale a prayer
and kiss the slick-skin of oily water.
A metamorphosis will make him rise,
hand on heart, through the dark.
Delicately he will slide up
onto the undulations of his new shore.

As the sun sets over Onagawa bay
he will unzip his pupate skin to the new air.
His wings will unfurl and creak dry
in the last drip of the sinking sun.
Full of new blood they will begin to beat
and he will rise on unseen ghostly eddies
into the kick and strut of his afterlife.

** In Japan, Yasuo Takamatsu is 64 years old. He goes diving once a week to look for his wife, Yuko, who was lost when the tsunami hit Onagawa, in Miyagi prefecture. He has been looking for her ever since. Mr. Takamatsu trained as a diver to try to find her. For the last seven years he has gone diving every week to look for her. So far he has completed 470 dives.*

DAN EGGS

## Tested In The Furnace of A Relationship

On the slope of a stony cliff-face of Rathlin Island there is an old pier
where cormorants dry their wings. On days when the water laps gently,
you can hear the kelp swish in the salt. Lilliputian shore bristle-tails
are woken by the smell of our trainers as we knot the rope to the half-broke rock.

“Go back to Dunseverick. Get kidnapped by the shrimps in the rock pool.”
we were ordered. At a dip on the slope, we stopped climbing, stood a while,
whispering into the bristle-tails’ ears, touching them. (They didn’t want touched.)
Did they weep on the chipboard of the skipper’s worktop?

Hellooo! We shouted at them and to the heavens we were sent, cheeks blushing.
Then we were hauled down, until the kettle sang and we circled the cabin dancing.
(That’s what any boat cabin is for.) The cormorants still dried their wings.
Gradient too steep for us to climb, but our love for them as constant as the Northern Star.

JAMIE FIELD

## Come Live With Me

Come live with me
and all the amenities we shall share
the water, the gas, on a quarterly/bi-quarterly basis
and all the appliances will be included in the rent.

The oven with the broken hob, the washing machine
made of damp, the toaster on its last leg,
and our housemates: Alun and his post-it notes,
Cahal with his three day benders.

Come partake in this borrowed joy and our living
will be cheaper, and we will know
the only thing we can own is each other's bodies.
as real as the box room we hide away in.

The shower we'll share with the hair of the German
boy who lived here for a week. Listen to the bangs
and clangs of Cahal wrecking the house again.
My love, let's stay in bed where it's safe.

VIVIANA FIORENTINO

## A Summer Place

[*windflowers*]

A summer many years ago
we stepped backwards into the river.

We smelled flowers, sweet amaranths,
above a patched sky's fast open and close,

your fingers painting
on the surface of water.

The rye grass bowed to the ground, offerings
to the millions of tiny organisms.

On the river bank
blue-eyed grasses anemones

aspens poppies waved promises.

Anemones, Pliny said, talk in the wind,
and aspen trees too.

For they are singing the absence of what
they've seen.

Invisibly we too made a promise,
buried unfinished moments

for the underworld is still living on,
remixing the layers, composting life.

KIT FRYATT

## Blades

honey

strop your edge
on my crop

harvest me
home to the last hag

fit guy like you
should leave

your hair
shirt off

an ex voto
nearer (my *god*)

to a queen
stroking down

a bona bobby shaft
(*oh*) you were reared

remember *the dock*
7 brian goldilocks

we were sounding
everyone out

we pelted
up the quays

lay on the boardwalk
clone spoons

ready to play
clatter together

heads bent
for a baazzer

(*baby*) be my beanie
in the baltic air

shield my scalp
from the stone-

splitting sun
my succour

my slim
shady garden

my desert rose
bud

my pearl
flood

my wadi

*after Muiredach Albanach Ó Dálaigh (fl. 1213-28)*
*on cutting his hair with Cathal Cródhearg*

CRÓNA GALLAGHER

## Achill 1972

On winter nights such as this
when iced air is cold as glass
and the blood of the sky a dark, galactic ink
you would take us outside in our bare feet
point north to the heavens, and instruct.

We used whale bones for stools
as you hedgerow taught, pinpointed the stars,
gave co-ordinates, latitudes and meridians,
the mapping terms from lost shipwrecks
that lie still under rock studded seas.

We would turn our faces like satellites, up
to find the warrior, to build it up from dots
until a giant of a man with rapier and holster
stood firm in Hibernian firmament.

Rivets and bolts formed an iron-age plough.
We would find the archaeological remains
and dig it out of the dark, so it could turn once more
the sods of night sky as a dash of startled milky way
was flung across the blackness
as seeds from a sack.

Then we'd stand in our pyjamas to go inside,
one of us slightly taller than the other, slightly older.
Another, slightly smaller and younger and another again.
This human staircase stepping up towards your lofty world
and you, the rudder on our round blue planet
turning 'round our cosmos, turning every tide.

CATHERINE GANDER

## Matches Ghazal

Working through a regiment of dull-headed sleeping soldiers to
find a willing match,
I smell a ship, a bed, a damp house. Such heat cast by a life
measured match by match.

It begins in the rare books aisle: a request, then an invitation. On
the pavement, we watch
noonday traffic yawn. You pull two cigarettes from your pocket
and I offer you a match.

Small talk, wine, homemade ragù, more wine, then surrender,
lubricant, your bed
a mattress on the floor. Locked bodies confuse the moves made in
a tango and a match.

Late summer evening in a beer garden, drunk, you slam down
your pint glass, smack
foam from your mouth and announce I could be good for you,
yes, even a match.

What noises now, on a sedate suburban night? At the end of
Catherine Road, a willow
dips her fingers in black ink. The wind hisses through them like a
suddenly spent match.

We strike, fail, strike, it doesn't catch – the gesture is too timid or
too strong. Which
person's story to believe when at sunrise the bruises on each
partner's body match?

ANGELA GARDNER

## Passage

the body loose
as a field, blue – offset in shadow, green – already lost
and beside this body another. at rest or not
: sinew and nerve, action
in its starting point. *I do not know why*
*it was beautiful.*
a breaking through and a falling away.
what may survive the rough winds of winter
the sunshine and rain. how easy the slope
misleads us, down to the sea.

TRACY GAUGHAN

## I've made an end of asking

I've made an end of asking for your love.
Since you made a tundra of mine, my heart
has shallow roots. The landscape here
is frozen much of the year and the wind
blowing through my dreams is incapable
of supporting them. My hopes lie close
to the ground. I suffer like lichen
on the heath, growing by breaking.
Desire in abeyance, I am a dormant sun.
I make no more battle for you, only
an end of asking.

MATTHEW GEDEN

## Zeno's Paradox

*after Lu Chi*

It will rain tonight or snow
and in the waiting hours bamboo
leaves rustle up your exquisite name.
Magnolia blossoms blush pink on grey
a defiant flag in this unceasing squall
of ferity; once great cities fall,
destinies cut down with no thought
of you and I watching different birds
wheel in the same starry sky.
I dream a letter but you are far
away so I fire a poem across
dynasties, half the distance
travelled each daily round, so love
flies on through endless life.
It will rain tonight or snow.

SONYA GILDEA

## Hope Street, Dublin

*Reading Miłosz, remembering Heaney*

Trying to eat with one hand
so as to read with the other
I am struck
by a sense of things here.

I am thinking, without form,
of love –
love, more precisely, in a time of war
and what it becomes after,

how to measure it –
its worth, yours, or my own?
how
to send on for word –

I am novice, and yet
I recall shifts of love
so sudden, so blinding
on afternoons made ordinary in light.

Some days I need this to matter
more than it can
and on days like these
I read instead.

RAY GIVANS

## The Way She Moved

I remember the green wheelbarrow
you were pushing the first time I saw you.
It was a common or garden construction.
You say you never pushed a wheelbarrow,
so, the head cover that ballooned up
like a chef's hat didn't exist, nor the black
wellington boots coming to a halt
half-way up to your knees. Every time
the subject arises you say it was another girl.
I am sure it was you, face sprinkled with freckles,
stars over the roof of The Stables.

JACKIE GORMAN

## I Thought of Those Captive Birds

A hotel room at 5am in New York,
your hands chasing mine in the half-light.
I thought of those captive birds in Helgoland acting out patterns of migration.
Northern Wheatears putting on weight, facing south and flapping their wings,
as scientists observed them in cages.
The sheets were warm and flimsy, as my hymen once was
when it was quickly broken.
In the way that a forsenic artist builds a face from a fragment,
a body can build a different sense of itself from just one day.
A still point of joy mingled with the fur scent of your neck,
sweaty from driving in New Jersey.

Hours later, I walked alone to the Natural History Museum.
At the Alaska Brown Bear Diorama,
through the glass I could sense their primal warmth.
I felt the hotel room key warm in my pocket
and wrapped my fingers around it.
In the giftshop, I bought a Hokusai print from the album
*Ehon tsui no hinagata* – models of couples.
Sparse lines, her head thrown back, curling fingers and toes,
entanglement and golden light.
Only yesterday, I noticed the expression on her face.
Then I remembered how the young man in the museum shop
blushed when I handed him the print
and looked straight into his hazel eyes.

ANGELA GRAHAM

## Just Friends

How cool it is tonight. How cool.
I hardly see but hear clearly
the sway and rush of grass;
dark bushes blot the green hem of the sky,
the river gleams
and I could drink that moon
– cool on the tongue it would
be, cool and curved.

My arms are full of roses, spiny and frail,
petals that drop at a breath.
Wild roses can't be hugged
– their stems collapse, thorns break –
so I hold carefully tonight
and can extravagantly praise
all this,
not you,
who stand on my left too close,
not close enough.

MARK GRANIER

## Crown Shyness

> *... a phenomenon observed in some tree species,*
> *in which the crowns of fully stocked trees*
> *do not touch each other, forming channel-like gaps.*
> —Wikipedia

If you want to see the pattern that they've made
you need to look up from the forest floor
in summer. Ends of branches don't abrade

each other, but leave ripples in their shade,
as if they've grown wary of that war
that moves inside the pattern that they've made.

Mapping the movements of the winds that flayed
and thrashed their heads till they became heart sore,
they made room for whatever might abrade.

It took time. Now the channels are inlaid
and every shivering tip has taken score,
moving in time with the pattern that they've made.

Seams in the brainy dark, a bright cascade,
a shyness almost human at its core,
a canopy of gaps that can't abrade;

no matter how many arguments have swayed
the trees, the wood — the gap between the door
and frame describes the pattern we have made,
that only stillness and silence will abrade.

EVA GRIFFIN

## Romance Option

*for Mícheál McCann*

How else would he know my intentions
if not for the cursor blinking over *yes, god, yes*
in some biblically horny way only the unreal can provoke.
My eyes on the screen; this life of fox fur and stolen gold.
The delay as the words fall from his mouth,
the slight blur at the corner of *you* and
*save a dance for me?* No matter. I relent.
What good is love without some metric for approval?
Easier to sit here and stalk an ending, line by line.
I talk and he has nothing new to say, despite
the camp sitting rich with spoils from the hinterlands.
Another quest. Him, silent. Each day I return, ask
*Was there something you needed?* He glitches
right to the lonely core of me: *Not at present.*

RICHARD HALPERIN

## Bird

A brown bird lands on the snow
of Lady Murasaki's garden.

I think the bird is Irish but how can I know?
She is not thinking of that.

She is thinking of the bird. On the snow.
It hops briefly, then is gone.

She is thinking of her husband who died recently.
Whom she loved. Whom she loves.

That she misses him is not how to express it.
Every night the moon is somewhere

whether she can see it or not.
Words like presence or absence

are out the window.
She is a writer. She knows this.

Stroke stroke go her brush and ink
of an evening. About the Emperor's court.

About the moon. About the Buddha of Mercy.
About the fact, and not necessary to say it,

that words are twigs, that ink and blood
and water and snow and hopping and weeping

are just the hem,
if that, of the garment of speechless love.

I am a writer.
Everything she writes including all of *Genji*

is a love poem to her husband.
Tell me it isn't.

## Modern Day Flowers

I had run out of toilet paper but
Before I realised
You had bought me more
Ultra-quilted.
Luxurious layers.
Three ply, the good shit.

RACHAEL HEGARTY

## Stonewall

Somewhere on a bog road, by a stonewall,
a woman can kiss another woman in winter
and together they can magic up the spring.

Then everybody can see, remember how
old stonewalls in Connemara play host
to all sorts of living things come the spring.

For small mites the wall becomes an eco-
Ballymun in the March sun and a nesting
place for loved up sparrows and wagtails.

The summer side is home for campanula
while the shade offers a limestone bed
to bare red lichen and a moss so velvety

it makes a dog dream of autumn pillows
as two women chat, laugh, stomp into winter
and kids play. All dance to the end of love.

In the pot, a soup is flavoured with rosemary
and creeping thyme hewn by brave warriors
somewhere on a bog road, by a stonewall.

RACHAEL HEGARTY

## Balla

Ag pointe fé leith ar bhóthar portaigh, lámh le balla fuar,
tig le bean bean eile a phógadh sa gheimhreadh
agus le chéile tig leo an t-earrach a mhúscailt trí draíocht.

Ansin beidh gach éinne in ann fheiceáil, in ann cuimhneamh ar,
conas a bhíonn cumas ar bhallaí fuara i gConamara
chuile sórt neach beo a óstáil le theacht an earraigh.

D'fhineoga beaga déantar Baile Munna éiceolaíoch don bhalla
fé ghrian an Mhárta, agus áit neadaithe
don ghealbhan 's don ghlasóg ag déanamh suirí.

Tá taobh an tsamhraidh ina bhunáit do scornlus,
an taobh faoi scáth ina leaba aoil
do léicean lom, do chaonach chomh síodúil san

's go gcuireann sé gadhar ag taibhreamh ar a philiúr fómhair,
beirt bhan ag comhrá, ag gáireadh, ag greadadh isteach sa
gheimhreadh,
páistí ag spraoi. An saol mór ag rince chuig céim dheiridh an ghrá.

Sa phota, tá an t-anraith blaistithe le marós,
agus le tím 'bhíonn ag leathadh, é bainte ó bhalla
ag pointe fé leith ar bhóthar portaigh, lámh le balla fuar.

*Aistrithe ag Theo Dorgan*

CLAIRE HENNESSY

## Purse

The phone in silent mode,
so there is no ding, no clink, and there should be –
your texts drop in like gold coins,
reassuring and solid in a velvet pouch,
the weight proof of worth.

AIDEEN HENRY

## The Shared Quotidian

On the whole, I prefer the nonverbal,
the softened look, the harsh hold,
the lightened or withheld caress.

The body can lie also,
to divert, embellish
or diminish.

But less circuitous than the mind,
the body is more instinctive in its truth,
the cover more likely to slip.

It can express
the mind's wish,
but fails to hide its own.

*I love you, I want you,*
may have some truth in it,
or not.

Two hands cradling the base of your skull,
drawing your lips in to a kiss, says everything
in that moment, promises nothing in the next.

*There's nothing wrong,*
*I'm good, we're good,*
an aspiration
with the possibility of cover-up.

Whereas a dearth of habitual touch, a paucity of eye contact,
diminished interest in the shared quotidian,
all suggest that we're not.

GUSTAV HIBBETT

## Rococo

ornamented into motion, like a dancer paintbrush-cast in costume
in the background of a *fête galante*, like the way you wake up
into dreams,
i'm *somewhere* without knowing how i got here. clouds fluffed pink,
skies as sinuous and rolling as they are in fresco. taken by surprise
and i'm still finding bearing; from here, the pastel fields of lavender
seem to stretch forever, all directions. *trompe l'œil* breeze – real, now,
as brush on gessoed canvas – warm against my cheek.

and what i mean by this, all this, is that i'm lucky – these days,
when i find my world falling, this is always where it lands.
some nights in dreams, i see your lilied figure spread above me
on the ceiling, a better place's favourite goddess. a deity who
always answers
prayers, with ears for only mine. in the blue and holied seafoam
of your eyes,
in the early morning trumpets of your voice, i find my absolution.
just,
i need for you to understand the way it felt for me to be nowhere,
and then – with you – such a rosy, stunning *somewhere*, suddenly

KEVIN HIGGINS

## Winter Coupling

He was a knock knock knocking cough
to which most of a man
was still theoretically attached.
She was as anxious as a cat
with arthritis in its elbows, thrown
among the pit-bull pups next door.
That solstice, it had been so long
since they'd tried intercourse
they had to use a Ouija board,
and employ a strange lady from Moravia,
dressed all in harlequin green,
to guide their papery, grey hands
zero to nine across it,
and commune
with the spirit of their springtime.

CATHERINE HIGGINS-MOORE

## Farrago

I line up all the things you gave me
like buns in a bakery window, placing
the cheap beaded necklace and fingerless
gloves in the back row. I examine the love

letters first, reading your relentless capitals.
Roll my eyes at Biro drawings. A stick-man
with arrows stabbing his broken heart. How
could I have thought a boy of twenty-two

could be a husband? Or me, a Gerbera daisy,
pressed between the folds of a New York City
map, could survive on mixed CDs and long-distance
calls? I kept our naked photos for years. Before

the movers come, I rip them into Scrabble squares
flutter them down the trash chute like confetti.
I wouldn't want someone to take Elmer's Glue
and fix us back together. Better this way. In pieces.

Forever separated. A strong wind, like the one
that blew up my skirt in Harlem, can't throw us
into each other now. Surely nothing can do that.
Not with all these miles between us.

## Always

No less now than then
is the light that falls across the river
florentine –

No less now than then
are the pillows that catch dreamflakes
snowlines –

No less now than then
can ambered figments
serpentine –

No less now than then
can eagle-hooded eyes
mesmerize –

No less now than then
can glance Vermeer
guillotine –

No less now than then –
Not more then than now –

## Soundings from a Hart

Another night of no sleep. 3 a.m.
and the house groans with shy souls
skirting the halls. We drop our gaze
as we pass, accepting this co-habitation.
In the kitchen, my dogs raise their heads
but do not rise when I slip out into the night.

The yard sheds its familiarity – outhouses
huddle on the cobbles, stones clutch stones
as ghost horses whinny in the empty stables –
their iron hooves paw decades of lost ground.

Curved above me the firmament is a miracle
of star-songs – Andromeda, Cassiopeia, Perseus.
I walk through darkness framed by winter oaks
that bend towards me in a bony embrace.

At the pier I sit, listen for the lake laid under
an expanse of black silk – so still I hear it
listen back and I wonder how have I fallen
so deeply out of love with life.

Yesterday I walked beside my friend –
we'd put his mother's ashes into the earth,
talk was of her days and her joys, when another
falls in, says – *I see you're walking alone; may I join you?*
It is never one thing that makes the black dog bark.

Something stirs and shears the bolt of silk –
dark water surges and wakes to the shore
where an antlered-stag steps inside the night,
so close I see stars undrown in his eyes,
sense love is a hart's rendition of the word love.

** Hart: a male red stag.*

LIZ HOUCHIN

## drinking tea in the garden after a sleepless night

if you were here now for the first time
on this June morning in those faded
jeans with the split knee and the t-shirt
with tour dates for a broken band

you would run your thumb through the bristly crown
of the Japanese pine and call it a bonsai pineapple

laugh at the fat wads of glaucous leaves bursting
from the gnarly trunk of the once dead whitebeam

lie on your belly on the uncut grass watching rivulet
moths mate on a stem of yellow rattle

steal the first Indigo Rose tomato from the cracked
greenhouse and bite it like a big black cherry

we would stay in the garden until nightfall breathing
honeysuckle
tuberose
jasmine

because now that you are not here
I think I finally understand
how to make you stay

## Oceanus

It's still on my mind,
the seaside Airbnb
that couldn't contain the raw thrill
of our undress and touch
like we were holy salvage
or in the midst of a feeding frenzy
and how other lovers may have had the best of us
but you tried and foamed and lashed your body to mine
as the Irish Sea battered on the door.

And it's still on my mind,
the condom lying like a wet mermaid's purse,
our heart urchins pulsing,
of how we laughed
when we came to leave
and couldn't find your phone
until we found it washed up in the tide of sheets,
and I felt the tow of you
as we swam up into the sun.

VIRGINIA KEANE

## Under Ruined Temple Michael

Should we bury it on the cliffs we walked
each New Year's Eve at midnight?

Or the park where we pushed our daughter's pram,
watched her learn to walk, feed ducks, climb trees?

Should it be on Sunset or on Hollywood Boulevard
where movie pioneers mixed memories with martinis?

Ballysaggart woods, the smell of leaf mould,
sausages cooking in our blackened camping pan
on twig fires beside a slow stream under beech trees?

Or under ruined Temple Michael by the Slaney estuary
drinking coffee from a flask without a notion
that love could ever be a corpse in need of burial?

BEN KEATINGE

## The Folly of Kočo Racin

In star-crossed Veles his love songs
scrawled themselves, drunk texts
to Rahilka, so radiant, blonde.
He was a pain until he left,
joined the Party, jail, death.

And yet, his poems were kept
carefully, in a biscuit tin,
oddball, Serb, strange, Bulgarian.
His real name was Kosta Solev
but hers was Raca, he became Racin.

## Zenith

We were rescued by the sun again
On Montjuich's verdant slopes.

I was covertly making a craft
Unnoticed by you, its timbers came

From the blue-white shimmer
Where water sweated into sky

And noon hit zenith
As we took on gold.

## Zenith

Agus an ghrian ár slánú an athuair
Ar fhánta uaine Montjuich.

Bhíos i mbun dáin
Faoi choim, a chasadhmad casta

Ó ghlioscarnach ghormgheal
Sháile íor na spéire

Is ar uair ard an lae
Seo chugainn an bonn órga.

SUSAN KELLY

## Long-distance Days

There was a sense of unease
a shuffling of feet and thoughts
as he stood in the doorway wondering would she come?
Snow polka-dotted the night.

When she left for Australia twelve months ago
they vowed to write letters, one a month,
she used eye-peeling neon envelopes
acid green, yellow, pink and orange in rotation

he used brown ones with windows from the office
and would type her address after he wrote the letter
sometimes not placing it correctly so an odd word was visible,
sometimes he did it to amuse the postman.

In between the relevant and ridiculous news
intimacies were laid bare,
they exposed themselves in ink
and it fuelled their long-distance days.

These two and three page microcosms of the other
were unfolded and re-read until a new missive arrived,
a closeness and a distance developed with each passing letter.
None had arrived in December.

CLAIRE-LISE KIEFFER

## So much of love is spent waiting

Waiting for you this evening, knitting, I too
am a Penelope weaving for her Ulysses,
stitch after ruby stitch bringing me closer to you,
my love. And though this room is no Ithaca,

the storm outside blackens the thuya
into a passable Ionian Sea,
an island of leaf green caught in the beam
of a streetlamp-turned-lighthouse.

Oh that you may arrive before the night is over
so I can finish my work without undoing,
and I dream of wearing my red pullover,
knowing, while dreaming, I won't have the words

to spell the weave of evenings, waitings,
dropped stitches of a love that is already waning.

HANNAH KIELY

## the stanza breaks are killing me

i write of her and wish she was here: *a woman i know*
of waking her with a kiss as i sit on the edge of an empty bed
of shared longing, and a hunger
of cracks and crevices of her body, asking *will you sleep with me*

i write of the quietness of my thoughts in a pandemic
of no sounds to contradict as the evening closes in
of the now silent piano unplayed, scales gathering dust
of art and the dwindling collection that is my memory

i write of a sky of stars and think of you
of a road unknown where i was lost
of my mother as she falls off the page
of street games in my childhood village

i write of sitting in a car, parked, waiting
of grief pumping my pulses
of scars and blood and wounds that won't heal
of virginity, endurance and early loss

i write of secrets between your thighs
of a girl i loved when i was just a girl
of rain and wind and storms and strangers
of sun and sea and lovers and *she*

i write of leaves that speak her name as they fall
of dirt in my fingernails as i work the soil
of dancing at dusk on a deserted beach
of winter melting on the mountainside

i write of a love letter i didn't send
of death and friends and the graves we cannot visit
of geography and maps and *you* in this atlas of time
of history and patience and shattered lives

i write of missing you and waiting for this to be over
of love that speaks louder than thunder

i write of the time we can no longer be together apart.

## Playing House

We play at it:
marriage.

You fix my son's hat
when it slips over his eyes
as he introduces you to the moon
that peeps from behind bruised clouds,
like an old friend who's been missing.

We don't admit that you know me
better than my husband ever did
or that I love you, in any way at all (we pretend.)

While I soak the smell of your
sleep(less) hot sheets from my skin,
you read about pirates & diggers,
fix shakily broken cranes,
the boy stuff I fail to understand.

I get quotes from the classics stuck in my head
as if they were lines from power ballads
blasted in the car.

*Beginning and end this abyss the sun and other*
(shut up!) dramatic shit like that
which possessed me
when I was young and committed
to the act of loving.

We don't stay out late like we did
years ago,
rushing back to relieve the babysitter.

You pull the bins down to the main road,
load the dishwasher while I rock a sobbing toddler.

A child in the buggy, your arm slung casually
over my shoulders. What could be more normal,
to a passer-by, than a young couple out
for a late-night walk, pushing a fretful kid?

It's nice, the roleplaying.
You perform your duties well,
make jokes about your hoodie being husband material,
close the cupboard doors when I leave them open.
I laugh unselfconsciously, remind you to drink enough
water to ward off the hangover.
We know, now, the trick to love
is not looking it in the eye.

My hand on your jaw, your back,
yours on my thighs,
I watch your pupils dilate as I come.

It's so nice, playing make-believe.
Later, over clink of kettle and pots, you say,
*This is nice, is this what it's supposed to be like?*
I freeze
in case the house falls down around me.

BRIAN KIRK

## Belturbet Under Frost

*for my parents, Terry & Anne*

I marvel at the flawlessness of things,
his shiny shoes, kind words, the cap he tossed
in her direction, and the songs he sings
that take him back. Belturbet under frost
those winter mornings when he'd leave his digs,
visit her shop before the Belfast train –
the street in darkness still – to purchase fags,
but really to see her. He can't refrain
from idling in the warmth of her shy smile
while the gruff owner indicates the time:
'Shouldn't you be on your way this while?'
He lingers by the door as the sun climbs
over Kilconny Bridge and rushing Erne.
The stations pass; she waits for his return.

SIMON LEWIS

## After Meeting in a Nightclub

We shared a box
of garlic and cheese fries
that first night, soaking
up the salty goo
of half-melted cheddar mayonnaise.
It must have been the garlic –
that unrefined spice.
We were stinking roses
in a garden of polished bollards,
manicured couples and orange lamps
and this midsummer night
had the sweetest taste.

AOIFE LYALL

## This page

Here –

I am giving it to you
to fill a picture frame or push
into the toes of wet boots
to balance a table or keep out
a draught

Here –

to tear apart for art or bookmarks
or to give purpose to a magnet
on a fridge, to make a shopping
list or to pick up crumbs, to top
with drops of nail polish or stripe
with fallen food

Here –

to light a fire or catch a spider
to keep count, keep score, to fold
in four and tuck away because love
can be hard to hold. Whatever you use
this love for, use it. I am giving it to you

Here –

NOELLE LYNSKEY

## Love Made Visible

in an exotic recipe for our breakfast:
oranges, limes, lemons, grapefruit,
the erotic kumquat on the table.

Our heads lean in, we peel
the outer layers, the knife
deftly cutting strips, fine to coarse,

peelings bed under fingernails,
the flesh smarts from an old cut
as we squeeze the juice,

feel it flow between our fingers,
holding out hands, we lick the drips,
then press the last of it into the pan,

wait while pith and pulp and brazen pips
come to the top, steeped in a muslin
sack. In a slow steam,

the scents simmer, the punch of rinds
perfumes the house with summer,
as clean as fresh bed linen. We'll savour

the bite of Five Fruit Marmalade,
a slow-cooked morning kiss, and us –
a harvest riper than all that fruit.

SEÁN LYSAGHT

## Epigram

*after Goethe*

They say that an epigram is too short
To say something of the heart.
But isn't a kiss even shorter?

CATHERINE PHIL MACCARTHY

## Summertime

I walk the meadow,
slip inside to see him read
stripped to the waist,
a silhouette of curls, his chest
crying out to be stroked.
The black cat tiptoes from his feet
arches its spine, brushes past me,
before our eyes meet

and suddenly we can't move.
His voice is a green belt of trees
after rain and we stand close,
talk about swimming,
and the view from a low window,
his heart under my hand
slowing to a purr.
There's an unmade bed,

a white sheet twisted over blue
that we unravel together.
How warm his skin,
despite cool linen
and the French windows open
all afternoon bringing stray voices,
even a curlew's call,
to the stillness of our room.

JOHN MACKENNA

## And

the clouds evaporated above Eros
and the sky became one wide, blue banner
and waves pebbled the low shoreline
and cicadas went on rehearsing their chorus
and, at midday, the red rocks came into focus
and the small birds slept in the great heat
and shadows tightened, vanished and grew again
and whitecaps dropped into the solemn sea
and a pair of wild horses came down the mountainside
and nuzzled your brown shoulders
and silence swallowed everything.

JIM MAGUIRE

## Shopping Centre Carpark, January

Once there was a scholar who needed to be an activist
who climbed the alder path to the hermitage
and did ten thousand bows.

Once there was a misanthrope who needed not to be a drunk
who found jewels on the rocks
where the Master's ashes were strewn.

This windblown Coke bottle in the Aldi carpark today,
made of hemp
and a gourd from a mountain pool

it has rolled directly out of the heart wearing full ceremonial robes,
like a head monk's attendant, rackety

fits of alacrity.
Like the clatter of tearooms, too hot sun,
your laugh. The wound

of an Irish sky in January – and the tissue-wrapped anchorite
you gave me, carved
into the darkness of her yonic cave –

who I thought I'd lost and found just now in the glovebox,
unrecognisable in her habit of dust.

MÍCHEÁL MCCANN

## Romance Option

*for Eva Griffin*

I direct my avatar in circles and rings
around the desires of a bohemian mage who
addresses me handsomely and hotly as 'thou'
or 'I blush as a stream bleeds red at sunset
seeing your figure appearing in my chambers'.
I hope to impress and make myself necessary,
and just for now I am the only one who knows
that I am pursuing a lithe man, that a world

trembles – uniquely mine – sealed by incantations
and decisions that *will be remembered later*.
The evening birds peep blearily in the loud hedge
of forest flame, and that I play at myself in secret
is no concern to them, and I return to enchanting.
Praise these vessels, rafts to a peopled island.

JAKI McCARRICK

## Scarecrows

*after 'Scarecrows at Newtownards' by Dan O'Neill,*
*at the National Gallery of Ireland*

We were looking at the Mournes,
at how they shadow Cooley,
when we got stuck;
we just seemed to dig deep
into sea-bog.
Then someone came and dressed us.

It was he that lives alone
in that wee house by Omeath,
with its back to the sea.
He dressed me in a blue skirt,
red scarf, put a bonnet on my head –
brown with stiff yellow ribbon,
wired in. Then buttoned on
these long green rag-tailed gloves.

At first I felt like Ruth
'amid the alien corn'
and I fell often.
Each time he oxtered me up,
spittle-cleaned my cheeks,
and the ravens left.
Then I weighed in and down
and was as good as home.

Now, in the greyest squall,
I stand tall and proud,

my skirt a prayer of hope
in the cornfield.
But I can't look at him when he comes.
My skull is not set on right,
is tilted towards Carlingford.

My sisters say that lately
he's been generous with silk,
is less contrary.
Well, my heart leaped at that.
The wire pinched.
The wind went through me
as through a disused byre.

## I'll Love You Till Sunday

Then I'll love you till Sunday.
And maybe we'll find each other on the streets of London
In the middle of winter,
Or at the first sign of spring.

And if your eyes still look into mine
The same way they do under London streetlights,
Under Manhattan skies,
Maybe I'll love you another day.

But for now,
I'll love you till Sunday.

Because you can hear it from the hills,
I know you can.
The early morning bells never cease to quiet,
Yet our hands never cease to wander.

You know as well as I,
Our love is meant to be seen only by moonlight.
Maybe I'll choose not to care this time.
There's always another way.

But for now,
I'll love you till Sunday.

KATHLEEN McCRACKEN

## Alaska

I wanted you to see Alaska
the snowpeaks & the timberline

but the work got in the way

I wanted to get my license, drive you north
to Tobermory, Manitoulin, Kapuskasing

but I failed the test

I wanted you to give up salt & sugar
cigarettes, red meat, the Jack

but life was hard enough

I wanted you to try tofu
Kombucha, ginseng, essiac

but old kicks trump new tricks

I wanted to stop the radio, physio, chemotherapy
the prescriptions, the injections, the predictions

but none of it was mine to call

I wanted you downwind of wildfire
outsmarting sparks, shooting the breeze

but I'd lost track of how to pray

I'd have walked on too but there was weather
        the fences needed bucking

& you were headed for the coast, the salmon boats
        crewed up and pushing out

                I wanted you to see Alaska

                I wanted you to see Alaska

KAREN McDONNELL

## Let Us Lie

Old soul, guarded as ever.
No social media for you.
The photo, an online happenstance.

Leave that black and white day.
Come here.
Kick off your shoes
and I will say to you,

Let us lie together.

We were at our best then,
facing each other.
Come to bed again.

You see greying roots at my scalp,
crinkle-skin on my hands.
I hear the crack in your voice but –

You haven't changed. Nor you.

I pinch my belly, you pat your paunch.
We lock eyes, laughing
at those selves and these; time-travelling
through a gaze and interlocked fingers.

Old heart.
Let us lie
together.

AFRIC McGLINCHEY

## This is our body

Sometimes, your eyes seem as brittle as the clouds,
following the wind's translucent flute.
But when you pull off your shirt,
one flowing movement,
a tremor glides over me,
an ecstasy that's almost holy.
This is my secret. You are my bread
and wine and chocolate.
I am your fortunate prisoner,
dressed in flames, burning all my ships
with the night's ignition.

On the beach, we lean, like two Pisas,
and I fasten to you, as lichen does to rock.
All that water, mobile space!
When I tell myself it's safer to need nothing,
an icy hand gropes the shadows,
finding only fear to clutch on.
Although I'm the unquiet one,
I keep silent about what's precious.
Then you turn to me, your glittering consciousness
erasing all the chasms I've created in my mind,
and love becomes a fire in my throat.

ELIZABETH McINTOSH

## Epithalamium

Is love a ring between us or a rope
around us, are our souls bound by steel?
Could it be cut, forged, or altered by time
like the wires ambitious men, greedy men,
laid across the ocean, connecting us?
The first transatlantic telecom cables
are still there, enduring the mystery
of unexplored depths. And sometimes,
even though they've long since been replaced,
those old cables are dredged up by mistake
when the lines need fixing. I thought marriage
was a fixed thing, but we were always
balancing on a hope which whispers in the dark
*do you still want me? Of course, yes.*

ALAN McMONAGLE

## After a Day

After a queasy morning searching uselessly
for the source of the mystery stream
that trickles towards the harbour-end of the canal
where water once ran red
and seagulls linger about the blind man
tossing crumbs from his loaf-wrapper;

After a wayward afternoon seeking comfort
inside the dungeon atmospheres
of the alley bars, chiding each other
with swarthy tonics and clink-clink tributes
to the day we take on the murder-hill over which
thunderclouds hover like tormentors;

After a torturous evening mostly loitering
by our cooking pot wondering, this time,
will we conjure a semblance of the flavours
breezing momently through our broken window
from the side-street bistro, while taking turns
at mangling each other's toes during our kitchen waltz;

After all of that we limped into the night as far as
the unlit pier where we held ourselves
in the black chill until, at last, we stole a glimpse
of Aldebaran and the winged horse cantering
across the restless firmament.
Off to bed with us then, and we slept like spoons.

LAUREN McNAMARA

## A Quaint 2016 Article

The headline read
'Best friends for 70 years'.
The interviewer asked 'what's
the secret to long life'?

They replied
'no men and a good friend'.
The article showed photos of
the house they owned together.

It was cheaper that way
and a picture of their room
with twin beds
and marks on the floorboards.

## Our mint-flavoured lips kindled

one another as we drank white Cuban rum.
By the third round, we were dancing
to a beat fast as a revolutionary song.
The bar's loo was a modest version of the Amazon Forest:
green-tiled floor and grass-green walls merging
with a dwarf banana tree and its waxy leaves.
Outside, eclipsed by thick halos of tobacco smoke,
a pinkish-red cathedral and a plaza:
bottles of wine clinking, different rhythms of laughter,
and tanned youths ready to fall in love.
Summer solstice celebrations all over the city:
each body shining like the blast of a thousand suns.

KELLY MICHELS

## Litany of the Human Heart

This is the heart.
The heart that can kill us or let us live
according to its whims. The heart

that knows the word for *abandonment*
in six thousand, nine hundred and nine different
languages, can recite the etymology for the word, *hunger* –
turn the five stages of grief into seven

while turning every face of heaven
toward it like a small sun.
It's the broken heart
inventing its own vocabulary from a sleepless night.

The heart that makes an anagram
for every empty gesture, finds a plastic bag
in the street to be a sign, the twisted
branch of a tree, an omen, the sting

of a paper cut, a prophecy. The moonstruck
red-eyed pendulum
of a heart. The heart that tells you to *let go*,
*move on*, to *go on ahead*

without it, that it will catch up eventually
but never does.
It's a compulsive hoarder
of a heart holding on to everything, like the pajamas

of a firstborn still laced with the scent
            of cornstarch, the sound of a loved one
breathing when asleep, a card someone sent
            for no reason if only to say

you are not forgotten, and all the other small
            veiled prayers flickering like fireflies
under the cupped fingers of night.

GERALDINE MITCHELL

## Late Nesting

*for S&J*

A week before midsummer's day
near Portobello Bridge
a pair of moorhens worked intently,
deaf to the din of traffic
or feet and laughter on the sunny bank.

One sat on the emerging nest, the other
brought the means to build it:
single strands of water grass,
sleek ribbons chosen carefully,
pulled up with a deft tweak of beak.

Journey after journey
in devoted concentration
the grass plucker came and went.
With equal application the other
wove, tucked the slender blades
around and under it.

Silent complicity, quiet confidence
of knowing, finding ease of love
when others thought they'd left it late.

## Uncharted Waters

How it started:
confessions
the naivety of
Christmas
in an inbox
to cling to
to a dot
past trenches
doldrums
uncharted
All this time
marooning us
But you know
there were four

small, pure things
in a day-lit bar
words arriving like
morning
life-rings
rip tides to carry us
on the edge of the chart
marked Duty
of Wifedom
white space.
I blamed you
old fool!
as well as I do:
hands on the wheel.

LUKE MORGAN

## Tattoo

Mum always maintained:
before getting one, print out
a picture of it, Sellotape it to your arm,
arse, belly-button, wherever,
and go about your life as normal
and if, after two full weeks
(including showers, washing all areas
of the skin except this,
the thin paper curling in the steam)
you still liked the look of it,
still rolled back your sleeve
between phone-calls to steal a quick smile,
then go for it. So,
I printed your face and taped it
to my forehead, and everywhere I went
every car window I passed
I put you through the silent test
before the ink could set into my raised pores,
before the colours could fade
and my skin could turn from raw pink
to stretchable again.

PETE MULLINEAUX

## x

Throw it, plant it, exchange it –
a quick peck, or a smacker
lips are essential, tongues optional,
mouth to mouth the general rule, although
cheeks will do –
from a distance you can blow it;
sometimes, during it, you might sigh –
releasing endorphins, oxytocin, dopamine,
serotonin, adrenaline; wet or dry,
always good for saying goodbye,
sealing a promise,
a mark of tenderness on the forehead;
other times it's just for show – kiss-kiss
or once a year under the mistletoe …
best slow …
a few you'll never forget;
Rodin sculpted, Klimt painted
but enough of this,
the pucker muscle
is orbicularis oris,
rhymes with bliss …
x

GERRY MURPHY

## Symposia

*after Plato*

We are on the beach,
I am facing the ocean,
you are behind me.
Your arms tight
around my midriff,
your chin digging in
between my shoulder-blades,
your breasts pressing
into my back
with sweet persistence.

I'm face down
on the bed writing.
You, face up, reading,
are filling
the long curve
between my shoulders
and lower back
with deft completion.

The separated halves
of our original whole
slotted together at last.

## Night Walk, Sláidín

Pebbles, tide-tossed, huddle on strands of net and seaweed smell,
shine
as if they had been dipped into that curved white bath of an
Imbolg moon.

I'd love to climb up, jump belly-first and splash in light, instead
of witnessing
the East Wind slap a sheep skull senseless with a beached
Domestos bottle.

Dripping home, candescent, I'd brighten Cúilín. You'd see me
glow outside
as I warm within, at the sight of you, drinking tea, in our lit
kitchen window.

CHANDRIKA NARAYANAN-MOHAN

## Donegal

A tree grows inside me,
from the diaphragm downwards, topsy-turvy,
with branches reaching for the soil below my feet
and roots that wrap around my ribs.

The spiders breeding in my belly are in my hair again
tangles of fuschia and black
growing and crawling through my insides
making me fuzzy, languid,

distracting.

They scuttle down bark, across new shoots,
weaving a home amongst the leaves, the moss,
the dark warm peat,
where I have allowed myself to be consumed,
just for you,
just this once
*(more than once)*
because this nightmare is comfortable,
and love is a velvet tree
that won't let me breathe.

## Dís

gal ónár mbeola
mórshiúl díse chuig carr reoite
ar champas tréigthe
fiacla seaca i mo scornach –

geallann breochloiche do shúl
dúlasrach dom
cadás na reoghealaí i mo bhéal

## Pair

steam from our lips
a parade of two to a frozen car
on an abandoned campus
frost-teeth in my throat –

the flints of your eyes
promise me dark flame
the moon's cold cotton in my mouth

## An Práta Deireanach

Baineadh siar asam nuair a thug mé suntas don líne
caol dubh faoi d'ingne. Créafóg na bprátaí luatha a
bhí á mbaint agat nuair a bhain lann speile an Bháis
an t-anam asat gan choinne.

Chuimhnigh mé ar do shíorcháiréis. Sobal na gallúnaí
ar an scuab ingne is tú do do sciúradh féin ag doirteal
na cistine. *Is den ghlóir an ghlaineacht* a deirteá.
*Ná fág aon jab leathdhéanta.*

Rinne mé athchóiriú ar an bpaidrín ach ní fhéadfainn
mo mhíchúram a cheilt. Ghabh mé leithscéal leat is
ghuigh go mbeadh báisín is sobal gallúnaí romhat ag
geataí na bhFlaitheas.

Agus lucht comhbhróin imithe abhaile nigh mé
gloiní is gréithe na sochraide. Amach liom sa gharraí.
Sheas mé os cionn leaba na dúlach inar luigh tú seal
sular íslíodh isteach thú i do leaba shíoraí.

Bhailigh mé na mirlíní prátaí isteach i mála
plaisteach. Tharraing mé chugam an tsluasaid is
rinne mé an uaigh oscailte a líonadh. Ní fhágfainn
an jab sin leathdhéanta.

Thug mé an mála beag leathlán iseach chuig doirteal
na cistine. Rinne mé na prátaí a sciomradh go séimh.
Gach líne dubh créafóige glanta, sciúrtha sular leag
mé le cúram iad i dtóin an phota.

ÁINE NÍ GHLINN

## The Last Potato

How did I miss it? The thin black line under your
fingernails. Clay from the drill of early potatoes you
were harvesting when the grim reaper came out of
nowhere and harvested your soul.

You were always so fastidious. I remembered the
soap suds on the nailbrush as you scrubbed and
scraped at the kitchen sink. *Cleanliness is next to
godliness* you'd say. *Never leave a job half done.*

I adjusted the rosary beads around your fingertips but
couldn't hide what I had already missed. I could only
apologise and pray that there would be a basin of
hot soapy water waiting at the pearly gates.

When the last of the mourners left, I washed the
glasses, scrubbed the kitchen clean. Then out to the
garden where I stood over the open ridge where you
lay awhile before being lifted into your final cot.

I gathered the scattered marbles into a plastic bag.
Picked up a shovel. Then, thud by hollow thud, I
filled in the open grave. This was one job I wouldn't
leave half done.

I brought the half-filled bag to the kitchen sink. I
scrubbed and scraped with care. Gently removing
each thin line of clay before setting the potatoes
in the bottom of the pot to boil.

Tharraing mé cathaoireacha is bord isteach cois cónra. Mias na bprátaí eadrainn mar a bhíodh gach lá le daichead bliain. Rinne mé scéalta an lae a roinnt leat. Ba dheas tú a bheith liom don suipéar deireanach.

Agus gan ach práta *la verguenza* fágtha d'fhéach mé i dtreo an fholúis ar do chathaoir. Ní fhéadfainn. Chaith mé súil i dtreo na méise. D'fhéach mé arís ar an bpráta deireanach. Ní fhéadfainn. Ní fhéadfainn.

Ní le teann náire ach le teann cumha a leag mé an práta sin ar phláta. An pláta scoilte sin a mbíodh dúil ar leith agatsa ann. Leag mé go cúramach sa chuisneoir é. D'fhéadfainn slán a fhágáil leat amárach, a stór.

I pulled the chairs and table up beside the coffin. The
dish of potatoes between us as it always was for the
past forty years. I filled you in on the events of the day.
It was good to have you there for one last supper.

When there was just the one old maid's potato left I
looked at the emptiness of your chair. I couldn't do it.
I looked at the dish. *La verguenza*. The potato of shame.
I couldn't do it. I couldn't.

And not from shame but with a heavy heart, I put that
last potato on a plate. The cracked plate you couldn't
bear to throw out. I put it tenderly into the fridge.
Goodbye could wait another day, my love.

*(* Note:: la verguenza [the shame] is the last slice on the plate – the old maid's slice that nobody wants to be the one to take).*

LANI O' HANLON

## TOUCHED

> *... as moonlight, but breathing.*
> —*The White Tiger.* R.S. Thomas

Last night it woke me, a thimble of light cutting
through the slit in the curtain, on your side of the bed.

You slept on, unaware of its still nesting
like the white sea glass we found on Curragh strand.

But it must have affected you all the same;

two hares rose up in the field beyond,
a vixen cried out, her throat full of moon.

I touched the silver thumbprint on the back of your head.

JEAN O'BRIEN

## Love Needs

There needs to have been a winter, harsh and
extraordinary, where you stripped down like
a leafless tree, your branches black and bare.
Your heart needs to have been emptied and spare,

hollowed out and waiting. You need to have
grown resilient and strong, to have re-
grouped, be sanctuary to your under-song
and gathered yourself to your true self again.

You need to become home to your own heart.
Then when spring inches in, you need to leaf up,
green out and flourish, tender, wild and strong.

Your heart needs to blow open with blossoms,
scatter buds like fat drops of rain, you need
to feel March winds, those April fevers.

TREASA O'BRIEN

## Winter in Costa Rica

The llama de bosque's burst flames have yelped
To the ground; spent lovers, they rest and glow

The banana tree's single bloom peels petals from herself
A striptease to help bananas grow

Bamboo sheds his dull stubble, and reveals
Green strokes on his hard yellow glare

A mariposa's wings so delicate one feels
A spider may have weaved her in the air

And all this green a different green to the green I know
I cannot break it with a stare and yet it lets me know

As the rain steals my breath into her hair
How can I be alone, when she is there?

## Thin Air

Her tied back hair the only colour as
she ushers the black and white striped
herd out of the lean-to into the passage,
*how how how how, how how how*
*how* … an octave above the sound
of the males in the parish, so it carries
in a morning air that's thin. Tilts her
brow, *how how how how, how how*
*how how*. A note that echoes in the next
townland, and beyond in a place where
the air is such, that people can talk from
hill to hill. Like in the Alps, where they
*yodle odle odle odle oh.* A lingo to sound
the other out, to suss who you can ogle.

NIAMH O'CONNELL

## The Dishwasher

The dishwasher is done.
Steaming glasses and shining cutlery.
I unload it, stacking plates in the cupboard.
A puddle sits on an upside-down mug, I turn
it over too fast. The splash on my foot is warm
and wet. I blush, thinking of the wet warmth
that fell on my thigh, except you're not here
to kiss me as it cools.

NUALA O'CONNOR

## The Red Massey Ferguson

He styles her Blessed, Beloved,
straddles her, to feel her exquisite torque.
When she won't turn over, he wheedles
in tones a spinster might use on a cat:
'Whisha, come on, girl, be good now.'

She thrums to life and he pets her flank,
sits like a lord on her buckeye seat
and savours her judder beneath him.
After spinning up the boreen to the field,
they furrow, penetrate the earth's cushion.

On Sundays, they waltz out together to Mass,
a scarlet woman and her biddable man.

MARY O'DONNELL

## Jukkurpa

You took the risk of wanting
to know me, a horde of awkward words
tumbling from the plain of my tongue,
when you tried to kiss me.
We hadn't yet learned
translation skills, though your tongue
awakened soon enough
to the salt of my estuarine travels,
nights when the sky's black dome
held sprinting stars above our bed.

At high tide we floated free
above the bioluminescence,
lit from beneath by neon blue.
Out in the swollen waves your desire,
a lit arrowhead on my thigh.

We forsook the shore to the beat
of a fast car. I pointed inland,
to a spirit-place out on the bog,
beyond the peat stacks.
There, we watched stippled trout
in a brown gully, penetrated the current
with a cautious finger after dusk,
for the ancestor trout to tickle against,
passing wisdom and pleasure.

Forty-five years by that bank,
and water-song to loosen
the lodged thorns we carried.

Rowan leaves and oak,
we marked with semen, blood;
a crow the flock had picked on,
now sacrificed,
gift to our time and all time,
written in the yellow sunset,
black bog ditches.

And what did we learn? Everything.
Nothing.
Outside time, that other world
droned busily
in the wheeling pits of the hours,
beyond us.

** Jukkurpa: Dreamtime, in the Warlpiri language*

JAMIE O'HALLORAN

## Out of the Gutter, into the Frame

I am a child of my age. It's a split age
where opposites attract like iron *schmutz*

to the magnet comb that lets me coif
the bald man in the cardboard toy. I forget

what I want to remember, but am plagued
by memories, like I'm a field and they're

a cloud of locusts eating winter's store.
Dust rains in my eyes. Gravity flies in my face.

What I let drop bounces back into my grip.
All the tired analogies crowd me –

butterflies, setting free, nevers meant to be.
What I attract is everything I have

abandoned until I stand, helpless pin,
bowled down by the lucky strike of love.

JUDY O'KANE

## Readers' Night at the London Review Bookshop

*This isn't a lonely hearts column,*
it read, *It is an occult ritual*
*that opens a gateway to hell itself.*

I set up camp in Travel.
A man drinking red wine disappeared
into History. We stood our ground

staring at the shelves.
The bell over the door rang out:
we were open for business.

I followed a high-pitched
frequency audible only to dogs.
Pair-bonding began.

I circled the room (invisible).
Sea salt crisps
crunched out loud,

contorting my face;
they made perfect little bowls
for the peanuts.

I leafed through Wine,
Biography and Poetry,
abandoning half-drunk

glasses on the shelves.
I devoured peanuts
using the crisps as shovels.

I headed home
in the company of an old faithful.
I was taking a refreshing

turn about the room with Miss Bennett
as the Tube pulled into Covent Garden.
A tall figure asked, *Is this seat taken?*

We stared ahead
as station names flashed by,
as the train hurtled into the night.

NESSA O'MAHONY

## Love in the Sixth Age

*'The sixth age shifts*
*Into the lean and slippered pantaloon'*
*—The Seven Ages of Man,* William Shakespeare

We took our vows,
and now between us
we comprise one decent body.
My shoulder takes the load
while you apply heating pads
to a throbbing muscle.
Your right wrist can twist
any jar lid imaginable,
when swollen joints
make my grip questionable.
My legs keep pace
with collie pulls
and hill slopes.
You see the small print,
when my squint
proves too faint
for detail.
We have one breath, too,
which you exhale
as I lie in the dark
holding mine,
counting insomnia's minutes.
Your ragged metronome
keeps beat with
the ringing in my ears.

## Loaves

*after Brendan Kennelly*

We have not yet met
though we're in the same place:
these things take time.

With nothing to contain us,
we spread ourselves
to the limits of free space.

My crust pushes towards
yours – this heat stretch –
till there's nowhere else to turn.

With our expansion
complete, the only
option now
is to yield
to the inescapable kiss.

*Note: A kissing-crust is the portion of the upper crust of a loaf that has touched another loaf in baking*

RORY O'SULLIVAN

## Sonnet

To me you are like a cup of coffee
  and a cigarette at half-past seven
in the morning on a dry day. Even
  now, like on a windscreen, you pour on me
with a kettle and melt the frost of all
  the everyday things which had covered
my face so I can see the uncovered
  sense of things. You are like alcohol
with sugar and weed cooked with butter
  and cocaine with less rammed intensity
and acid with less fear and ecstasy
  with more calm and ketamine with softer
drips without waking lonely in the glare
  of guilt and thirst and vomit and despair.

LOUISE OMER

## st germain boulevard

pain au chocolat and black coffee on the gold-ringed table
number 115; at café de flores where patti smith
wrote about devotion. australia on the phone: on friday

there was a plate of oysters and an orange sun of prawns,
gemma said we feast on the carcasses of unworthy men.
all deaths should be celebrated because they taste of birth.

at the next table a model with floating blonde hair
sits schoolgirl straight and i pretend the photographers are
looking at my morning curls. the thought of a cigarette thrills

i light up and read maggie nelson on love; before 9 a.m. i took
photos of my round arse in the mirror of my broken room,
of the cello of my torso, spine like an empty river.

love? i once loved a man who was a soldier trained to kill

in paris it is romantic to smoke. a suited security guard strolls
rue saint benoît outside the louis vuitton store and its quietly
    obscene
suitcases; sun in my eyes, october air nibbles between

ankle boot and rolled denim cuff; the photographers abandon
scattered plates and the model crosses the road in high heels
again and again each time fresh in cold morning's promise sharp

nicotine thrums and trust is my odyssey
so many unworthy men left an ashtray in my mouth
one thing has died another born

but maybe i'll have another café allonge
this might be the day i see patti smith writing
and she can tell me
the true meaning
of devotion.

RUTH QUINLAN

## Mothlight

He smoothes the creases from her forehead,
feathers away crow's feet with the pad of his thumb.

When she lies on her stomach, he counts vertebrae
up the abacus of her spine, writes words like *forever*

on the planes of her shoulder-blades;
she smiles, pretends they're true.

When he sleeps, she studies him in moonlight,
pulls the sheet aside to envy the grace of limbs

that do not yet function as barometers,
aching to predict the slide of winter.

She marks the beat of his unworn heart
wishing, by force of osmosis

that her own cautious timekeeper
would measure life this unflinchingly.

She marvels at the mothlight of his youth, prays
that he will never leave, that she will still survive,

alone in her kitchen when he does.

NELL REGAN

## You Are To Me

As basil scent is to fingertip,
illuminate to manuscript
and ballast is to cargo ship;

As slow burn is to charcoal,
reception to a mobile;
distraction to a two year old;

As honey is to raw throat,
China is to slow boat
and mp3 is to download;

As right change is to bus fare,
downy is to mohair
and ergonomics to office chair;

As milk is to steeping tea,
laughter is to levity
and conker is to gravity;

As oiled feather is to bird flight,
perception is to second sight
and earth-tilt is to day light;

so you are, to me.

MARY RINGLAND

## Salvaged

*for Terry*

We lie side by side; a cloud of damp languishes
on the ceiling above our bed. I tilt my head

and catch the outline of a man and his boat, quite distinct.
They are mottled brown, the boom idle, cleats stagnant,

the rowlocks empty like stapes unheeded. I nudge
closer to you and notice a speckled mound.

The man is with someone smaller, his wife I wonder,
there has been a night storm and loss, sculls adrift,

their coats sodden, the colour of old water,
their backs bowed from what they have tholed.

I shift to your side to hear their imagined murmurings.
They are face to face, their frosted breath sheer as a bride's veil,

a flask steadied between their feet; a small chrome cup
and salvaged tales passed to sweeten this harsh dawn.

TANVI ROBERTS

## We Do Not Speak Of Her

*'And after*
*the first minute, when I say, Is this about*
*her, and he says No it's about*
*you, we do not speak of her.'*
*—Sharon Olds*

For months they did not speak of me. I was vast and unarticulated
thing – χάος, as the Greeks meant – more chasm
than chaos. I was unseparated gloop
of stars, mighty zygote, verb unparsed,
threads not yet unpicked. Slowly, slowly, I sharpened
into vision: dream antelope
at carlight. They were breaking up like
voices and I was not guilty, but
I was implicated; I was in court
every day watching them; I was between
the clauses of law and underneath his
nails. I was not happy
but I could not stop
laughing, I was not sad but
I was crying. And suddenly I was real,
a god's thought turned being; as if
I had drunk the blood of her shade,
I was able to speak, and my body
was a thing to be touched – I was flesh –
and he was as if I'd wiped rain
from my glasses, only for them to become misted
with my own breath.

JANE ROBINSON

## Woven Boat

We have grown into each other,
our bog-oak limbs
polished as oar-shafts,
your elbow melding with mine.

We find ourselves
crammed in this coracle,
rocked out of the same substance
our bodies lost somewhere

while we lean to the journey.
Our stillness is extraordinary
as we balance one another
in this eggshell of a dream,

the storm in you roaring into me,
my flight leading you to symmetry.

MARK ROPER

## Usage

Too delicate to open, my father's bible.
The much-dented metal of a thermos.

Prayer flags, colours whitening,
cotton gently weathering away.

Patches of gold our palms have worn
on a bannister's dark brown rail.

The small roofless church in a field:
a grey mare, the vault beside it a foal.

Clean, bright edge of a spade,
the shine where it first enters earth.

In a cathedral, left on a post until
it turns to air, a cardinal's biretta.

Love, your hand in mine, all these years –
the use the world has made of us.

JOHN SAUNDERS

## Promise

*for MF*

The linden trees bend fluent in the wind
like penitents in prayer. Their leaves are hearts.
The parched grass is a blanket of soft skin.

This day is paradise, a hymn of unspoken wants.
How we soak up its essence, lick clean our fingers,
close eyes to pain and wash our souls in warmth.

We bury ourselves under branches of maple trees,
shelter throughout the winters of our years,
safe from the cold thief of happiness.

And now it's time for blades to rip the earth.
Seeds explode with the desire of multiplication
as we stand and watch the promise of new growth.

The cycle begins; tractors in fields mould furrows.
Our life is tomorrow, tomorrow, tomorrow.

SOPHIE SEGURA

## Reformer

For you these repetitions, three sets
of twenty at the bus stop, or while brushing my teeth.
For you this urging of private machinery to greatness.

Once desired, possessed, colonised, anaesthetised,
sectioned, now leaking mid-life's ichor, doesn't this body
deserve resurgence, a reacquaintance with potency?

The Spartans at Thermopylae, drilled in pankration,
used their mouths and bare hands once their weapons broke.
I too am capable of intimate combat, of empty-hand submission.

Oh, to demonstrate the internalised lesson, this willingness
for engagement! To dedicate my mornings on the apparatus
to holding the Teaser position and eye contact.

D'OR SEIFER

## Second Decade in Free Verse

Life isn't a cocktail party in the perfect vintage dress –
the moths ate that long ago.

Marriage isn't a moonlit walk on the boulevard –
leaves a gobo of mystery, the river gurgling at our elegance.

Our covalence is the metre of the mundane –
your snores filtered through the ceiling.

Our consonance is checking your ears for wax, inspecting
the corners of my mouth post coffee.

Our romance is a walk in Dublin after the rain
regressed it, freeing it from tourists.

Our scansion is your knowing the
cruxes I will reach (before I do).

An echo at the Spanish Arch,
you shoo away gulls while I eat chips, standing in a puddle.

You grant me your coffee dregs
finish my cooling *single*.

We share the crash of waves,
the shapes in cloudy skies.

JOHN W. SEXTON

## Hydrangeas

Looking out at them, exposed in the rain,
I feel the condemnation of my self-pity.
In the cold squalls they look gone, bereft
of their summer glories. Their many faces

like those of sodden, spectral contemplatives
awaiting revelation. Soon, their heads
will fall to the secateurs of March. It is all
so much, so much like the memories

of what we had, and had forever.
But forever seems finite now. Somewhere,
high above, a seam in the clouds
gives way, and light is abundant,

ubiquitous, playing amongst the ghosts
of those crowded skulls. And in that sunlight
I sense a foreshadowing of hope.
Later, having stepped outside, I notice buds

and furled pennants of green. The hope,
I realise, has held. It is like the light
of your voice from afar, playing
between the hurtful distances of our dormant

lives. For us, my love, are summers yet.
Not withering are we, just wintering.

## Out of Dazzle

The slope eased its summer limb into
the lake only to feel a drowned February.

*

A 13th century poem laid peace in two voices,
the book passing as gently as sieved flour.

*

Cardboard boats ferried words like 'your love
of adventure' towards the lost village.

*

A wagtail left a branch, jiggered
along the shore, pecking like rain.

*

We watched each boat float out of dazzle
caught in the personality of the wind.

*

Longing stayed light as the closed head
of a white tulip bought at a service station.

*

You could make that lake in bronze as a body
with a hand outstretched and it would not be sad.

*

Car boots opened for the market traders overcome
with substance and a scorching possessiveness.

*

The car snatched the sunset in a gold bauble
fast down the chorus of my loud motorway.

GERARD SMYTH

## Like Byron's Daughter

On the night of the eclipse she lured him
with her astronomer's knowledge
of Venus and the planets.
She took him to the observatory,
told him she could magnify the stars.

Their arrangement was to meet when the sun
went down, out Finglas way.
But the sky was charcoal with clouds of rain
and the promise she made
was impossible to keep.

Like Byron's daughter it was her belief
that science was making the old beliefs
obsolete, or so she said
that night they searched the Milky Way
but couldn't find her starry crown,

no primal flash among the galaxies
or comet's tail to read as augury
of the *yet-to-happen, what's-to-come*.
That night the sky was Dead End Street,
He wished her happiness and luck.

ROSS THOMPSON

## Princes Street Gardens, Edinburgh

Just before closing time,
we snuck
into the sunken park
where the dark,
a special kind of Scottish dark,
coated trees and grass
like the water
that once filled
this former loch
and for the briefest
of moments
we lost track
of the hour
and moved
like basking sharks
between the fibreglass
shards of Halloween
cold, the bitter
scent of spent fireworks,
hops wafting from the brewery
like the coming snow,
and the greenery
that shimmered
behind the air
like anemone and waterwheels,
and all the while
the words to express
how beautiful I found
this evening,
your mother and you

caught in my throat
so I wrote them down
on borrowed paper
as soon as we returned
to our hotel.

## Faint

*for M*

*Adapted from the HSE's website on fainting*

*If you are with someone who has fainted, try to keep calm.*
Of all things, during dinner I bite my cheek
right at the very moment it is on the tip of my tongue
to ask you to come live with me and be my person.

*If you can, lay them on their back and raise their legs.*
I kneel beneath you on a Reseda-green towel. You run
your hands through my hair and sit on the lip of the bathtub.
The sun streams through the frosted glass of the window.

*The person who has fainted should wake up within twenty seconds.*
One minute, you're stepping out of your morning shower –
the next, you are holding me from behind on the kitchen floor
confettied with green peas and pancetta. You tell me you've got me;

you caught me when I slumped, taking our weight
in a half-space between falling and lowering, one more time.

MORGAN L. VENTURA

## Wildness

In the bluebell-blossomed garden,
arrangements of life simmer. When I'm here,
I hear the amaryllis wish me vivid
and I find you under the ash tree
luminous in golden shadow, in bed
with such nectarine wildness.
If the hummingbird kept a diary
what would it say, save
for *thrum thrum thrum*?
What a tiny mighty heart
exploding like tender cumulus!
When I'm here, I hear everything bloom.
Bouquets of clouds saunter past me
and in your eyes, the fervent skies.

BENJAMIN WEBB

## Copula

I am the subject. I see couples coupled,
weighted perfectly as a balanced phrase.
Yearning is my copula: that my days
may kindle warmth, my nights be not so cold.
To be or – yes, to be; no *ors* and *whethers*,
I'll weather storms of slings and arrows,
I'll oar through troubled seas alone,
I'll learn to be content to be, untethered
from syntactic expectation. No predicate?
A subject being:
                                        but, up in the fiery absence,
darkness of space speckling unpaired footprints,
paths cross that blazed no less brightly separate.
Perhaps I'll be and find a predicate too,
each complement, though each in self complete: You.

GRACE WILENTZ

## Gift of the Magi

Waking with the tip of my nose
so close to a soft neck
with its delicate ridge of spine –
an ellipsis, a dotted line.

Carefully I crawl over and out of bed,
step to the bathroom where I meet
my blanket-creased face, and feel
the heaviness of last night's sleep,

and another sensation, too –
like I have lived a thousand lives
on this turn somehow forged
something beautiful out of a lot of bad luck.

It's my turn to make the coffee,
toast bread and melt cheese.
I open the window to get a read
on the day, lean into the air.

It's almost Christmas but being
from the North you mightn't know it
by the downpours and the heat
already rising from the concrete.

But tonight, between late evening and dusk
(call it *crepúsculo*) lights will come on
pink and green lining the windows
of the high-rises at the favela's outskirts.

At that hour I'll find myself here
as we make dinner side by side, a song
quietly playing in the background,
chopping beside steaming pots

of rice and beans and sharing a cool beer,
pulling spinach leaves from the stalk,
discerning fresh from wilted, and patiently waiting
for the bay leaf's slow, certain yield.

ANNIE WILLIAMS

## Oranges

how strange it is
to think of that sticky city –
lumpy city,
plucked-out-guts city,
bandit at the foot of the staircase.

how strange it is
to think of your eyes behind green glass –
the blood in the sink,
the smog, the *stink* –
do you remember him? our wretched guest?
do you remember how he wailed?

on the wall there is a photograph of you and me when we were lovers.

it is my birthday and i am wearing yellow and i am smiling up
    at you so wide.

how strange it is
to think of how the grime pooled in the grate
(the grubby lungs the wailer ate)
when i set sail for california.
do you remember how you looked at me?
do you remember how you laughed?

but oh! forgive me
how *sweet* it is, of course,
to slump beneath the sun with your book in my lap

*reading the lies that you have told*

and pretend that we were happy.

MILENA WILLIAMSON

## Untitled Nude

*for E*

*'No space must be regarded as great except the ocean.'*
—Edgar Degas

*'Do not forget that the exhibition is only two steps from the street corner.'*
—J.M. Michel

Once the space between us was as great as the ocean.
Now we sit close, eat mocha cheesecake at midnight,
sleep late and kiss goodbye, lingering on the street corner.

You ask if I lived an alternate life before we met.
I fall into the multiverse of girl-body-person-woman
with every text, floating or drowning between oceans

and yes, I have been catcalled. On the street, on the corner,
once, braless and running to Victoria Square for lingerie.
Afterwards, in a blue dress, I read poems in The American.

I do not want to be regarded by anyone except the ocean:
Barleycove, Coral Beach, Rosses Point, Kinnagoe Bay.
In Blackhead, we walk past the lighthouse, down the stairs

and sit on the rocks, eating steak pasties in the salty air.
The life with you is the one in which I am healed;
you kneel on a towel and I sit on the bathtub's corner.

Afterwards, I stand at the window in the dark kitchen
to drink water, eat a yogurt and fix my hair, still nude.
At every corner, I am a woman on a street corner.
Regarding myself (as you do), I am as great as the ocean.

JOSEPH WOODS

## Let's get lost

*'Let's get crossed off everybody's list'*
—Sung by Chet Baker

Who'd have thought from such beginnings
still together now after twenty years, despite two earthquakes
early on which had roles in bringing us together.
And not to mention that tsunami or its aftermath
that sent you scurrying off again. In the fourth year
of our marriage we choose to circle the globe
with all its consequences as if to make a vow
of restlessness or simply add to the sum of years
on the road. With our only daughter barely walking
we flitted first to toddler-friendly Burma
and after free elections, thence to Zim …
a few coups d'états later, we sit on the veranda
and exhale to evening shadows lengthening on the grass,
I reach for your hand, hoping we never settle.

ENDA WYLEY

## Great Big Bed

*'For one night only*
*naked in your arms.'*
—Beatriz, Countess of Dia, c. 1175

This great big bed
makes me think of you.
Not that I've ever lain
a full long night
with you before –
but if I could,
it would be here,
would be now,
in this great big bed,
the skylight overhead.

Slant of hail,
a blind of snow,
the whole world
fierce outside
and us within
breathless
in a storm of sheets –
the high triple mattress
a royal test of love,
our skin bruised
by the pea of desire.

But look, a small crack
in the glass
where weather
is spurting in –

oh, cruel observer
of what we're about! –
sleet to freeze our eyelids,
wind's bitter slicing
of our cheeks.

And then –
so slowly –
how a single flake
of snow
can drop
into your mouth
and melt
upon your tongue
that is busy
in its own way
melting over mine.

# CONTRIBUTORS

GRAHAM ALLEN'S (b. 1963) poetry collections *The One That Got Away* and *The Madhouse System* are published by New Binary Press, as is his ongoing epoem *www.holesbygrahamallen.org.*

JOSEPH ALLEN (b. 1961) was born in Ballymena. He has published six collections, most recently, *Clabber Street Blue* (Greenwich Exchange Publishing).

BEBE ASHLEY (b. 1995) lives in rural Co. Down. Her debut poetry collection, *Gold Light Shining,* is published by Banshee Press. *www.bebe-ashley.com.*

AMANDA BELL (b. 1968) is a Dublin-based writer and assistant editor of *The Haibun Journal.* Her most recent collections are *Riptide* (Doire Press, 2021) and *Revolution* (wildflower poetry press, 2022)

MAUREEN BOYLE was born in 1961. *The Last Spring of the World* was published by Arlen House in July 2022. She is a poetry mentor with the Irish Writers' Centre.

NICK BOYLE was born in Belfast in 1979. He is a composer, pianist and student psychotherapist with an MA in Poetry from Queen's University.

DYLAN BRENNAN (b. 1980) was a recipient of the Ireland Chair of Poetry Bursary Award in 2019. His debut poetry collection, *Blood Oranges*, was published in 2014.

ELLEN BRICKLEY (b. 1984) is a writer, heritage manager and grateful recipient of two Arts Council literature bursaries. Her work has appeared in *Banshee*, *Sonder* and others.

CHARLOTTE BUCKLEY was born in 1988 in Kent. Her poems have appeared in *The Stinging Fly*, *Ambit*, and *The Rialto.* She lives in Dublin pursuing a PhD in ecofeminist poetry.

PADDY BUSHE was born in Dublin in 1948 and lives in Kerry. He writes in Irish and English. His most recent books are *Second Sight: Poems in Irish* and *Peripheral Vision,* both from Dedalus Press, 2020.

DAVID BUTLER's (b. 1964) third poetry collection, *Liffey Sequence* (Doire Press), and second short story collection, *Fugitive* (Arlen House), were both published in 2021. He lives in Bray.

DARAGH BYRNE (b. 1978) is an Irish poet living in Sydney. His work has been published in numerous journals and anthologies in Ireland and Australia.

ALICIA BYRNE KEANE (b. Dublin, 1993) has been published by *The Stinging Fly, Banshee* and *The Colorado Review*, among others. Alicia's debut collection is forthcoming from Broken Sleep Books.

LORRAINE CAREY was born in 1973 in Greencastle, Donegal and lives in Kerry. Her poems recently appeared in *Rust+Moth, Ink Sweat & Tears* and *Bindweed.* She has been selected for The Stinging Fly Summer School 2022.

ANGELA T. CARR (b. 1970) is a poet and recipient of an Arts Council Literature Bursary 2021. Originally from Glasgow, she lives in Dublin. *www.adreamingskin.com.*

ANNE CASEY (b. 1967) is a native of west Clare and now based in Sydney, Australia. She is the author of four poetry collections and her work is widely published and awarded internationally. *www.anne-casey.com*

EILEEN CASEY (b. Offaly, 1956) is a Patrick and Katherine Kavanagh Fellowship recipient. *Bog Treasure* (Arlen House) and *Bogmen First and Last* (Fiery Arrow Press) are both recent collections, 2021.

LOUISE G. COLE (b. 1956) is originally from Worcestershire and now lives in rural Ireland. She won the Hennessy Literary Award for Emerging Poetry in 2018 and her pamphlet, *Soft Touch,* was selected in the Laureate's Choice series in February 2019.

SHIA CONLON (b. 1990) is an Irish writer/artist whose work has been centered around marginalized voices and growing up in the landscape of working-class Catholic Ireland.

STEPHANIE CONN was born in County Down, NI in 1976. She is the author of three poetry collections, all from Doire Press, including the recently published *off-kilter*.

EMILY COOPER was born in 1988. Her work has been published in *The Stinging Fly*, *Banshee* and *Poetry Ireland Review* among others. *Glass* was published in 2021 by Makina Books.

POLINA COSGRAVE (b. 1988) is a Russian-born poet based in Ireland. Her debut collection *My Name Is* was published by Dedalus Press (2020). Polina lives in Wicklow with her daughter.

DEREK COYLE was born in Naas, Co. Kildare in 1971. He currently lives and works in Carlow. His second collection, *Sipping Martinis under Mount Leinster,* is forthcoming.

ENDA COYLE-GREENE, born in Dublin in 1954, lives in Skerries. Her most recent collection is *Indigo, Electric, Baby* (Dedalus Press, 2020). She is co-founder and Artistic Director of the Fingal Poetry Festival.

BERNIE CRAWFORD (b. 1954) lives by the sea in County Galway. Her first collection *Living Water* was published by Chaffinch Press, 2021. She is a co-editor of the poetry magazine *Skylight 47.*

PHILLIP CRYMBLE (b. 1967) is a physically disabled poet from Belfast. In 2007 he was selected for Poetry Ireland's Introductions series. In 2016 his debut collection was published by Salmon.

CATHERINE ANN CULLEN (b. Drogheda, 1961) is an award-winning poet, children's author and songwriter. She was Poetry Ireland's inaugural Poet in Residence. Her seven books include *The Other Now* (Dedalus Press, 2016).

EMILY CULLEN (b. 1973) is the Meskell UL-Fifty Poet in Residence. Her most recent collection, *Conditional Perfect* (Doire Press) was included in *The Irish Times* round-up of 'the best new poetry of 2019'.

YVONNE CULLEN was born in Dublin in 1966 and now lives between her home city and Inishbofin island. She mentors writers and is currently writing on the overlap between her travels and the stories of Ireland's vanished travelling shows.

MARTINA DALTON was born in 1963. She lives in Tramore, County Waterford. Publications include *Poetry Ireland Review, The Irish Times* and *The Stinging Fly.* She received a Dedalus Press mentorship in 2021.

MAUREEN DALY was born in 1941 and lives in Dublin. She came to writing poetry late in life. Her poems have appeared in anthologies, in *Revival* and mostly recently in *Cyphers.*

PHILIP DAVISON was born in Dublin in 1957. He has published nine novels. He writes radio drama. His poems have appeared in various journals. He is a member of Aosdána.

STEPHEN DE BÚRCA (b. 1991), a PhD candidate at Queen's University, has work in *Poetry Ireland Review*, the Ireland Chair of Poetry's *Hold Open the Door*, and elsewhere.

CELIA DE FRÉINE was born in in 1948 Newtownards and now lives in Dublin and Connemara. Her most recent poetry collection in *Léaslíne a Lorg: In Search of a Horizon.*

PATRICK DEELEY, born in Loughrea in 1953, now lives in Dublin. Seven collections of his poems have been published by Dedalus Press, most recently *The End of the World.*

MAURICE DEVITT (b. Dublin, 1957) was a winner of the Trocaire/Poetry Ireland and Poems for Patience competitions, and published his debut collection, *Growing Up in Colour*, with Doire Press in 2018.

PATRICK DILLON's (b. 1956) publications include *The Café Review*, *Poetry Ireland Review*, Stedlijk Museum, *The Moth* and the *Echoing Years Anthology of Poetry* from Ireland and Canada.

MOYRA DONALDSON was born in Co. Down in 1956 and has published nine collections of poetry, most recently *Bone House* (Doire Press, 2021).

DARREN DONOHUE (b. 1975) is an award-winning poet/ playwright based in Co. Kilkenny. His debut poetry collection, *Secret Poets,* is published by Turas Press.

KATHERINE DUFFY was born in Dundalk in 1962 and lives in Dublin. Her publications include *Talking the Owl Away* (Templar Poetry, 2018) and *Sorrow's Egg* (Dedalus Press, 2011).

RORY DUFFY (b. 1963) lives in Athlone. His poetry has been published in *Hold Open The Door, Southword, Crannog, Ropes, Stony Thursday, Skylight 47, Boyne Berries* & others. He was a Forward Prize Nominee in 2021.

DAN EGGS (b. 1961) is a poet from Ballymoney, Co. Antrim, a stone's throw from where he now lives. His debut collection was published by Lagan Press in 2003. His work was been published in *Magnetic North, Emerging Poets* (Verbal Arts Centre, 2008).

JAMIE FIELD (36 yrs, from Pontefract, West Yorkshire) was selected for the Poetry Ireland Introductions in 2021 and holds a MA in Poetry from Queens University, Belfast.

VIVIANA FIORENTINO was born in Italy in 1979 and lives in Belfast. Some of her poems in English appeared in anthologies and were recorded for the Irish Poetry Reading Archive (UCD).

KIT FRYATT (b. 1978) lectures in English at Dublin City University. His most recent book of poetry is *Bodyservant* (Shearsman, 2018).

CRÓNA GALLAGHER (b. 1968) lives in Co. Leitrim and works as a Printmaker and Writer. Her written work has appeared in quality publications in Ireland and beyond.

CATHERINE GANDER's (b. 1977) poems have been published widely and internationally. She has a series of poems forthcoming with Nine Pens Press's NINE SERIES (2022).

ANGELA GARDNER is the author six poetry books. *The Sorry Tale of the Mignonette*, Shearsman Books, is a UK National Poetry Day recommendation for 2021.

TRACY GAUGHAN (b. 1971) is a writer and editor based in Galway. A 2022 Forward Prize nominee, her collective anthology, *Pushed Toward the Blue Hour,* is published by Nine Pens Press.

MATTHEW GEDEN was born in England in 1965, moving to Kinsale in 1990. His most recent publications are *The Place Inside* (Dedalus Press) and *The Cloud Architect* (Doire Press).

SONYA GILDEA is a Poetry Ireland Introductions poet (2021) and recipient of an Arts Council Literature Bursary Award. She is published in various journals and anthologies and lives in Dublin.

RAY GIVANS was born in Co. Tyrone in 1951 and lives in Belfast. *Tolstoy in Love* was published by Dedalus Press in 2009; he has also published a pamphlet with Poetry Salzburg, at The University of Salzburg.

JACKIE GORMAN was born in Athlone in 1971. Her debut collection *The Wounded Stork* was published by The Onslaught Press and her work has appeared in a number of journals.

ANGELA GRAHAM (b. 1957) is from Belfast. Her poetry collection, *Sanctuary: There Must Be Somewhere* (Seren Books) was published in May 2022. *@angelagraham8*

MARK GRANIER was born in London in 1957, and lives in Bray, Co Wicklow, with his wife, son and two dogs. His fifth collection is *Ghostlight: New & Selected Poems* (Salmon, 2017).

EVA GRIFFIN (b. 1994) lives in Dublin. Her pamphlets *Fake Hands / Real Flowers* and *one last spin around the sun* were published by Broken Sleep Books.

RICHARD W. HALPERIN, born in Chicago in 1943, is an Irish-U.S. dual-national residing in France. His poetry collections are published by Salmon (Cliffs of Moher) and Lapwing (Belfast).

CLODAGH HEALY was born in 1998 and raised in Kerry and is a graduate of Creative Writing at UCD. Her writing is heavily influenced by the mythical and mundane happenings of Irish life.

RACHAEL HEGARTY was born in Dublin in 1968 and is a poet and educator. Her debut, *Flight Paths Over Finglas* won the Shine Strong Award. Her *May Day 1974* and *Dancing with Memory* also earned critical acclaim.

CLAIRE HENNESSY was born in Dublin in 1986. She is the author of several YA novels and her poetry appears in *ROPES*, *Southword*, *The Lonely Crowd*, among others.

AIDEEN HENRY's (b. 1963) two collections of poetry, *Hands Moving at the Speed of Falling Snow* and *Slow Bruise*, were published with Salmon Poetry. She is finalising her third collection.

GUSTAV PARKER HIBBETT (b. 1996) is a Black poet, essayist, and MFA dropout. Originally from New Mexico, they are currently pursuing a PhD at Trinity College Dublin.

KEVIN HIGGINS was born in London in 1967 and lives in Galway. His sixth collection is *Ecstatic* (Salmon, March 2022).

CATHERINE HIGGINS-MOORE (b. 1984) holds degrees from Trinity College Dublin and the University of Oxford. She contributes to the *TLS*. Her play *Daniel* recently ran in Dublin and New York.

DEIRDRE HINES is a poet and playwright. *The Language of Coats* was published by New Island Books in 2012. She sits on the organisational committee of North West Words, an arts organisation that promotes new writing in Co. Donegal.

ELEANOR HOOKER's (b. 1963) latest poetry books are *Where Memory Lies* (Ponc Press) and *Of Ochre and Ash* (Dedalus Press). She is a PhD candidate at the University of Limerick.

LIZ HOUCHIN (b. 1973) lives in Dublin. *Anatomy of a Honey girl (poems for tired women)* was published by Southword in 2021.

ROSEMARY JENKINSON was born in Belfast in 1967 and is a playwright, short story writer and ACNI Major Artist. Her latest collection of short stories is *Marching Season* (Arlen House).

VIRGINIA KEANE was born in 1945 in Cappoquin and lives in Ardmore, Co. Waterford. She runs writers' retreats in her mother Molly Keane's house. She has been published in *Poetry* (Chicago), *Poetry Ireland Review* and *Washing Windows Too.*

BEN KEATINGE was born in Dublin in 1973 and educated at Trinity College Dublin. His poems have been published in *The Irish Times, Archipelago* and anthologised in *Local Wonders* (2021).

PATRICK KEHOE was born in Enniscorthy, Co. Wexford (where he currently lives) on St Patrick's Day, 1956. His most recent book of poems is *Places to Sleep* (Salmon Poetry, 2018).

SUSAN KELLY (b. 1974) is from Westport. Her work has appeared in *Cyphers, Poetry Ireland Review, The Stony Thursday Book, Crannóg, Revival, The Ogham Stone, Abridged, The London Magazine* and *Boyne Berries.*

CLAIRE-LISE KIEFFER was born in France in 1990, and lives in Galway. Her poems have featured in magazines and anthologies. She is an Arts Council Agility Award recipient.

HANNAH KIELY (b. 1959) lives in Galway. Her poetry has featured in *Over the Edge Writers, Vox Galvia – new Galway Writing, Spilling Cocoa over Martin Amis, Galway Music Residency* and *Pendemic.ie.*

ALICE KINSELLA was born in Dublin in 1993, and raised in Co. Mayo, where she now lives. She is author of *Sexy Fruit* (Broken Sleep, 2018) and *Milk* (Picador, 2023).

BRIAN KIRK was born in Dublin in 1964. His most recent publications are *After The Fall* (Salmon Poetry, 2017) and *It's Not Me, It's You* (Southword Editions, 2019).

SIMON LEWIS (b. 1978) lives in Carlow. His most recent collection is *Ah Men!* (Doire Press, 2019.) His first collection, *Jewtown,* was shortlisted for the Shine/Strong Award.

AOIFE LYALL (b. 1987) was born in Dublin and lives in the Scottish Highlands with her family. Her debut poetry collection, *Mother, Nature,* was published by Bloodaxe Books in 2021.

NOELLE LYNSKEY (b. 1959) is Director of Portumna's Shorelines Festival. She is currently completing her MA (Creative Writing) in UL and was selected as Strokestown's Poet Laureate.

SEÁN LYSAGHT (b. 1957) grew up in Limerick and now lives in Mayo. He has published several collections, including *Carnival Masks* (2014) and *New Leaf* (2022), both from The Gallery Press.

CATHERINE PHIL MACCARTHY was born in Limerick in 1954. Her collections include *Daughters of the House* and *The Invisible Threshold.* She received the Lawrence O'Shaughnessy Award for Poetry in 2014.

JOHN MACKENNA was born in Castledermot, Co. Kildare in 1952. He is the author of twenty-two books, the most recent of which are *We Seldom Talk About the Past: Selected Short Stories* and *I Knew This Place.*

JIM MAGUIRE was born in Wexford in 1962. *Music Field* was shortlisted for the Shine/Strong Award in 2014. He is currently working on a collection of poems set in Korea.

MÍCHEÁL MCCANN (b. 1996) is from Derry. A pamphlet of poems, *Keeper,* was published in 2022 by 14publishing. He lives and works in Belfast.

JAKI MCCARRICK was the winner of the Papatango Prize for her play Leopoldville. Her play *Belfast Girls* has been staged internationally. Her poetry has been published widely.

MAC MCCLUSKEY (b. 2002) is a deaf, queer poet from the US. He lives in Northern Ireland and his work is featured in *The Apiary.*

KATHLEEN MCCRACKEN (b. 1960) is a Canadian poet based in Belfast. She is the author of eight collections of poetry, including *Double Self Portrait with Mirror: New and Selected Poems.*

KAREN J. MCDONNELL (b. 1961) is from the Burren in Co. Clare. Her poem 'Driftwood' was shortlisted for Irish Poem of the Year in 2021. Her debut collection is *This Little World* (Doire Press). *karenjmcdonnell.com.*

AFRIC MCGLINCHEY was born in Galway and lives in West Cork. Her most recent publication is *Tied to the Wind* (Broken Sleep Books), a hybrid memoir about her nomadic childhood.

ELIZABETH MCINTOSH was born in California in 1994 and lives in Belfast. Her poems have been published internationally in *Image Journal, Poetry Ireland Review* and *bath magg.*

ALAN MCMONAGLE has published two collections of short stories, *Liar Liar* and *Psychotic Episodes*, and two novels, *Ithaca* and *Laura Cassidy's Walk Of Fame*. He lives in Galway.

LAUREN MCNAMARA from Doon, Co. Limerick is a poet, playwright and performance poet. She performed her most recent poetry play, *Hello My Name is Single,* at Glastonbury Festival 2022.

RAFAEL MENDES (b. 1993) is from Brazil. His work has been included in the Dedalus Press antholgy *Writing Home,* published in *Litro* magazine and archived on UCD Poetry Reading Archive.

KELLY MICHELS was born in Chicago in 1978 and lives in Dublin. Her work has appeared in numerous journals. Her most recent pamphlet, *Disquiet,* was published in 2015.

GERALDINE MITCHELL was born in Dublin in 1949 and lives on the Co. Mayo coast. Her fourth collection, *Mute/ Unmute,* was published by Arlen House in 2020.

AUDREY MOLLOY (b. 1972) grew up in Blackwater, Co Wexford, and lives in Sydney. Her debut poetry collection is *The Important Things* (The Gallery Press, 2021). She studies poetry at Manchester Metropolitan University.

LUKE MORGAN was born in 1994 and lives in Galway, where he works as a writer and filmmaker. His most recent collection is *Beast* (Arlen House, 2022).

PETE MULLINEAUX (b. 1951) lives in Galway. He's written plays for stage and RTÉ radio, and a novel. A fifth poetry collection, *We are the Walrus,* is due from Salmon in 2022.

GERRY MURPHY was born in Cork in 1952. His latest publication is *The Humours of Nothingness* (Dedalus Press, 2020).

KIERAN FIONN MURPHY (b. New York City, 1966) lives in Dingle. His poetry has appeared in *Skylight 47, Lime Square,* etc. He is currently studying writing at UCC.

CHANDRIKA NARAYANAN-MOHAN was born in India in 1988 and is a writer and cultural consultant living in Dublin. She has had work published by in the Dedalus Press anthologies *Writing Home* and *Local Wonders*, and in publications from UCD Press, Lifeboat Press, *Banshee* and others.

LAOIGHSEACH NÍ CHOISTEALBHA (b. 1994) is from Donegal and lives in Galway. She is working on her first poetry collection in Irish and is also an amateur artist.

ÁINE NÍ GHLINN (b. 1955) is a poet and children's writer and Laureate na nÓg (2020 – 2023). Born in Co Tipperary in 1955, her most recent collection is *Rúin Oscailte.*

JEAN O'BRIEN's (b. Dublin, 1952) sixth and latest collection is *Stars Burn Regardless* (Salmon Publishing 2022). An award winning poet, her work appears regularly in journals and anthologies. *www.jeanobrienpoet.ie*

TREASA O'BRIEN is a writer, artist, filmmaker and educator, living in Galway. Her work has been published by Routledge, Cambridge, Goldsmiths, Manchester University Press and Circa, Sight & Sound, amongst others. *www.treasaobrien.com*

EUGENE O'CONNELL was born in 1951. His poetry collections include *One Clear Call* and *Diviner*. A new book of poems, *Thin Air,* is forthcoming. He is co-editor with Pat Boran of *The Deep Heart's Core: Irish Poets Revisit a Touchstone Poem* (Dedalus Press, 2017).

NIAMH O'CONNELL is a Cork-based poet, born 1995. Her poetry has appeared in *The Quarryman, Bealtaine* and *Banshee Literary Journal.* She holds an MA in Writing Poetry from Newcastle University, having graduated in 2020.

NUALA O'CONNOR was born in Dublin in 1970, her fifth novel *Nora* (New Island), about Nora Barnacle and James Joyce, was a Top 10 historical novel in the *New York Times.*

MARY O'DONNELL (b. 1954) is author of eight collections of poetry and eight works of fiction. Her most recent collection is *Massacre of the Birds* (Salmon). She is a member of Aosdána.

JAMIE O'HALLORAN was born in New York in 1955 and lives in Connemara. Her *Corona Connemara and Half a Crown* was the 2021 Fool for Poetry Chapbook 2nd place winner.

LANI O'HANLON was born in Dublin in 1968, and is a dancer and movement therapist. Recent publication in *Poetry Wales, Portland Review, Orbis 200* and *The Amphibian Lit.*

JUDY O'KANE (b. 1969) is a poet and prose writer. She holds a PhD in Creative and Critical Writing from the University of East Anglia and lives and works in Dublin.

NESSA O'MAHONY was born in Dublin in 1964 and lives there. She has published five collections of poetry, the most recent being *The Hollow Woman and the Island* (Salmon Poetry, 2019).

MAEVE O'SULLIVAN (b. 1963) has published five collections with Alba Publishing, the most recent being *Wasp on the Prayer Flag* (2021). She leads haiku workshops, and reviews for various journals. *www.maeveosullivan.com.*

RORY O'SULLIVAN (b. 1997) from Cork, lives in Dublin and did a PhD in ancient Greek literature. He has appeared in places such as *Channel, Púca,* and *Skylight 47.*

LOUISE OMER (b. 1989) is a writer born on Kaurna Country, Australia, who has lived in Dublin and Galway. Her first book, a memoir and feminist critique of religion, is *Holy Woman.*

RUTH QUINLAN (b. 1975) is originally from Kerry but now lives in Galway. She has won awards for both poetry and fiction and is co-editor of *Skylight 47,* a bi-annual poetry magazine.

NELL REGAN was born in London in 1969. Her latest book is *A Gap in the Clouds: A New Translation of the Ogura Hyakunin Isshu* with James Hadley (Dedalus Press, 2021).

MARY RINGLAND (b. 1965) is from Holywood, Co. Down. Her work has appeared in *Washing Windows, Her Other Language* and *Washing Windows Too* (Arlen House), *The Bangor Literary Journal* and C.A.P. anthologies.

TANVI ROBERTS (b. 1999) calls Belfast her home. Her poems have appeared or are forthcoming in *Rattle, The Moth* and *Poetry Ireland Review*. She was longlisted for the 2021 National Poetry Competition.

JANE ROBINSON (b. 1962) lives in Dublin. Her first collection *Journey to the Sleeping Whale* (Salmon) received the Shine-Strong Award. A second collection, forthcoming 2023, includes the collaborative sequence 'For the Atoll'.

MARK ROPER was born in Derbyshire, England in 1951 and has long lived in Ireland. His latest collection, *Beyond Stillness*, is published by Dedalus Press in October 2022.

JOHN SAUNDERS was born in Wexford in 1956. His last collection, entitled *Chance*, was published in 2013.

SOPHIE SEGURA (b. Dublin, 1978) lives between Madrid and Buenos Aires. She is working towards a collection on, among other things, pilates.

D'OR SEIFER (b. 1984) lives in Limerick. Her poems have appeared in *The Waxed Lemon, Skylight 47, Abridged,* and more. She co-runs the online poetry series Lime Square Poets.

JOHN W. SEXTON was born in 1958 and lives on Carn Mór, just west of Kenmare. His experimentalist collection, *The Nothingness Kit,* is published by Beir Bua, autumn 2022.

CHERRY SMYTH (b. 1960) has published four poetry collections, a novel and two books of non-fiction. Her latest collection, *Famished,* explores the Irish Famine.

GERARD SMYTH is a Dubliner, born in 1951. His tenth collection, *The Sundays of Eternity* was published by Dedalus Press in 2020. He is a member of Aosdána.

ROSS THOMPSON (b. 1975) is a writer and Arts Council award recipient from Bangor, Northern Ireland. His debut poetry collection *Threading The Light* is published by Dedalus Press.

EOGHAN TOTTEN was born in London in 1993. He is a Longley poetry scholar at Queen's University Belfast, with poems in *Local Wonders: Poems of Our Immediate Surrounds, The Honest Ulsterman, The Apiary* & *Abridged.*

MORGAN L. VENTURA (b. 1988, Evanston, IL, USA) is a writer based in Belfast. Their work appears or is forthcoming in the *Magazine of Fantasy and Science Fiction*, *Abridged*, and *Strange Horizons*, among others.

BENJAMIN WEBB is from Castlerock, Co. Derry. He was born in 1999. From September, he will begin an MA at the Seamus Heaney Centre in Belfast.

GRACE WILENTZ was born in New York City in 1985 and lives in Dublin's Liberties. She is the author of *The Limit of Light* (The Gallery Press, 2020).

ANNIE WILLIAMS (b. 1996) is a PhD student and poet based in Dublin. She has published criticism, fiction, and poetry in *The Modernist Review, Berkeley Fiction Review* and *Yolk Literary Journal.*

MILENA WILLIAMSON (b. 1994) is finishing a PhD in poetry at the Seamus Heaney Centre. She received an Eric Gregory Award. Her debut pamphlet is forthcoming from Green Bottle Press.

JOSEPH WOODS was born in Drogheda in 1966 and has recently returned to Ireland after many years living abroad. He is the author of four collections of poetry, the most recent of which is *Monsoon Diary* (Dedalus Press, 2018).

ENDA WYLEY was born in Dublin in 1966. Her six collections with Dedalus Press include *New and Selected Poems* and *The Painter on His Bike*. She is a member of Aosdána.

LEEANNE QUINN was born in Drogheda and grew up there and in Monasterboice, Co. Louth. Her debut collection of poetry, *Before You,* was published by Dedalus Press in 2012 and highly commended in the Forward Prize for Poetry 2013. Her second collection, *Some Lives,* was published in 2020 and noted as a Book of the Year by *The Irish Times* and *The Irish Independent.* She is the recipient of three Arts Council Bursary awards, most recently in 2021. Her poems have been widely anthologised, appearing in *The Forward Book of Poetry 2013, Windharp: Poems of Ireland Since 1916, Hold Open the Door: A Commemorative Anthology from The Ireland Chair of Poetry,* and *Queering The Green: Post-2000 Queer Irish Poetry.* She lives in Munich, Germany.

JOSEPH WOODS is a poet, writer, editor and former director of Poetry Ireland. He returned to Ireland last year after eight years in Burma and Zimbabwe and is attached to the University of Limerick where he teaches and pursues a PhD. He was appointed director of Strokestown International Poetry Festival earlier this year. A former winner of the Patrick Kavanagh Poetry Award, he was twice a recipient of the Katherine and Patrick Kavanagh Fellowship and Literature Bursaries from the Arts Council of Ireland. In 2013 he was awarded the Irodalmi Jelen Prize for the Hungarian edition of *Ocean Letters* (Dedalus Press, 2011).

# ACKNOWLEDGEMENTS

Acknowledgements and thanks are due to the editors and publishers of the following where a number of these poems originally appeared:

BEBE ASHLEY: 'Sappho, who is doing you wrong' was first published in *Modern Poetry in Translation: Origins of the Fire Emoji* (Focus on Dead Women Poets); MARTIN DALTON: 'Because Her Wedding Had to Be Postponed' was first published in *Channel,* with thanks to editors Cassia Gaden Gilmartin and Elizabeth Murtough; VIVIANA FIORENTINO: 'A Summer Place' was previously published in *The Stinging Fly;* CATHERINE GANDER: 'Matches Ghazal' was first published in the June 2022 edition of *On The Seawall;* DEIRDRE HINES: 'Always' was first published in *Abridged;* CLAIRE-LISE KIEFFER: 'So much of love is spent waiting' was first published in *The Madrigal,* Vol. IV, 'Verity'; KATHLEEN McCRACKEN: 'Alaska', *Cyphers* 89; JANE ROBINSON: 'Woven Boat' was first published in *Skylight 47,* issue 11; MILENA WILLIAMSON: 'Untitled Nude' was previously published in her debut pamphlet from Green Bottle Press.

The editors would like to thank Aoife Lynch for all her assistance and support. Special thanks is due to Pat Boran for his idea and for initiating the call for poems and placing his trust in us as editors. Huge gratitude is also due to all of the poets who responded to the call for submissions with such open, interesting and generous writing. It's been an honour reading and engaging with your poems. — *LQ & JW*

www.ingramcontent.com/pod-product-compliance
Ingram Content Group UK Ltd.
Pitfield, Milton Keynes, MK11 3LW, UK
UKHW042020290726
14061UKWH00002BB/104